ESTATE PLANNING

for
Middle and Large
Income Earners

Save THOUSANDS to MILLIONS

of dollars through proper

estate planning!

Joy Casey

This publication is designed to provide accurate and authoritative information in regard to the subject matter covered. It is sold with the understanding that the publisher is not engaged in rendering legal, accounting, or other professional service. If legal advice or other expert assistance is required, the services of a competent professional person should be sought. From a *Declaration of Principles jointly adopted by a Committee of the American Bar Association and a Committee of Publishers.*

ISBN: 0-9641627-0-9
Trade Paper

Printed in the United States of America

What advisers and others are saying about "Estate Planning for Middle and Large Income Earners"

"It's rare to find a book written for professionals that's so concise, and easy to read, that it works just as well for clients as it does for their advisors. In fact, both advisors and insurance companies have purchased the book in bulk to distribute to their clients."

Robert Clark, Editor-in-Chief, Dow Jones Investment Advisor

"I recommend your manual to our agents for their use and the use of their clients. I have found the information to be very practical and easy to understand."

Stuart G. Tugman, CLU, ChFC, AEP
VP Advanced Sales/Mktg. Svcs. of Jefferson-Pilot Life Ins. Co.
Past President of the American Society of CLU & ChFC

"I definitely recommend that your manual be one of the client educational tools for every estate planner."

Jeffry F. Bahls, J.D., Estate Planning Attorney

"The information you provide is easy to use, well organized, and of real value to those individuals interested in preserving their estates from the ravages of estate taxes."

Terry Kaltenbach CLU, ChFC
Past President of California Life Underwriters Association

"Your manual was an 'easy read' on a difficult subject matter. Your work will help me personally as well as countless others who want to manage their money well."

Jeffry H. Blanchard, D.C.

"Introducing someone to estate taxes, gift taxes, trusts, and financial planning is a difficult task. Your book now gives me a resource to work with that keeps things simple, usable and brief."

John Stremlau, CPA

"Much can be learned in a short period of time by reading your book."

Wayne H. Winters, J.D., Investment and Tax Consultant

CONTENTS

Introduction:
Estate Planning

Part One:
The Problems

Part Two:
The Solutions

ESTATE PLANNING

"Bad news—our consultant says we're leaving most of our property to Uncle Sam and he isn't even in the will!"

Introduction

"Did You Purposely Name the IRS as the Primary Beneficiary of Your Estate?"

No? Then you should be aware of the fact that without proper planning, a huge share of your estate could wind up in the hands of the tax collector, a share that is often greater than the amount you leave your family. All told, large estates can lose as much as 70% (and even more) to taxes, legal fees and other expenses. Smaller estates face serious problems, too, even those currently under the Federal Estate Tax Exemption[1] (those with a net worth under $650,000) for they are still subject to the high costs and frustrations associated with probate. In addition, both large and small estates can run into serious problems and incur increased expenses as the result of many common errors and misconceptions. The solution? Estate planning!

Estate Planning — What Is It?

It is an extremely important type of planning designed to insure the successful building and preservation of your estate. The wonderful result of proper estate planning is that you will:

- **GIVE LESS** of what's yours to the government

- **KEEP MORE** of everything you are spending your lifetime to build and acquire; and as a result

- **SAVE** literally thousands to hundreds of thousands of dollars, depending on the size of your estate.

What is Involved in Estate Planning?

Estate planning is a two-pronged approach that looks to both the decisions you make during your lifetime as well as critical decisions you must make concerning the transfer of your assets at death. In addition, estate planning is two-pronged in another way in that the aim is to both:

1. Make you aware of some potentially very serious problems.

2. Provide you with the tools and techniques available under the law through tax, financial, and insurance planning to achieve successful, cost-effective solutions.

First and foremost, however, it is essential that you become alert to the fact that:

Without proper planning your estate may face untold thousands of dollars of loss unnecessarily, depending on the size of your estate!

Problems (frequently unanticipated) which left unaddressed, may have serious consequences:

- **Probate** — Potentially expensive; time delays. Average costs are approximately 5% of the GROSS estate with a value that exceeds $30,000 to $100,000 (depending on the state) in personal property and $10,000/$20,000 in real property. (Costs may be higher or lower than 5% depending on a number of factors.)

- **Death Taxes** — Heirs face hefty tax bills of 37% to 60% of a net estate's value over $650,000—due in nine months in cash!

- **Other Taxes** — You may not know about but which can greatly impact your estate!

- **Concerns Regarding Minor or Disabled Children and Other Heirs:**

  - Guardianship in the event of the parents' death.

  - Common errors which leave the rights of children unprotected. For example, accidentally disinheriting stepchildren, children from a prior marriage or your children if you or your spouse dies and the surviving spouse remarries.

- **Conservatorship** — *(Also known as guardianship in some states.)* Legal costs, annual accountings to the court, incompetency of the disabled adult is public record.

- **Long Term Care Concerns** — Annual nursing home costs range from $30,000 to $60,000 and more! Estate owners must *"spend down"* their assets to federal and state poverty levels in order to qualify for Medicaid.

- **Huge Pension Tax Traps** — Large private pensions can face triple taxation: income taxes, estate taxes, and possible generation skipping taxes.

- **Business Continuation Concerns** — Disruption of the business, including a possible forced sale or liquidation due to the death or disability of a key business owner or employee.

Commonly held misconceptions that lead to a false sense of security, such as:

- **Estate Planning is Just for the Wealthy.** Untrue! Many times smaller estates may suffer substantial losses without proper planning.

- **Estate Planning is Only for Seniors.** This is not true! There are many advantages to starting early. On the other hand, waiting too long will only limit your options. This is particularly true when you have assets which are growing rapidly either through inflation, acquisition and growth, or appreciation.

  By the way, two smart businessmen who believed in the value of early estate planning were Sam Walton, founder of the hugely successful Wal Mart stores and Malcolm Forbes, founder of *Forbes Magazine. Unfortunately, many other high-profile celebrities, statesmen, and business people were not so lucky and, at their deaths, suffered huge losses to their estates.* (See page 43.)

- **Having a Will Avoids Probate.** Absolutely untrue!

- **Planning is a One-Time Endeavor.** Not at all! Very serious problems can arise if you do not keep your wills, trusts, life insurance policies, buy-sell agreements (business purchase agreements) etc., up-to-date!

  For example, if you have a will or trust which was drafted prior to some very significant tax-law changes which occurred in 1981 and which you *have not updated,* your estate may face serious planning problems and may wind up paying MORE than its share of taxes!

- **Planning Can Be Put Off Until Sometime in the Future.** This is a very dangerous assumption for a number of reasons:

  - **You May Run Out of Time** —No one knows when he or she will run out of tomorrows.

  - **Your Family May Pay a Big Price** — Loved ones can face huge problems that they are ill-equipped to solve. Indeed, they could encounter problems on all fronts: loss of financial and emotional security; family conflicts over the disposition of the estate; critical business or financial decisions they are unprepared to make; and forced sales of family assets, etc. Whether the surviving spouse is elderly and perhaps in poor health or younger and struggling to raise the children, the lack of proper planning can cause much unnecessary suffering.

  - **"The IRS Giveth and the IRS Taketh Away"** — *Tools available to you now may not be available later.* In addition, some of the tools and techniques need to be acted upon in a timely manner.

    For example, both spouses must be alive to be able to take advantage of a very significant tax break. One tax credit currently available to married couples *allows them to save up to $330,000 (or more depending on the year of death of each spouse) off their federal estate taxes!*

- **You Don't Have to do Anything in Order to Get the Tax Breaks for Which You Are Entitled** —Absolutely untrue! the tragedy is that most estate owners do not realize that they stand to lose ***thousands of dollars by not claiming their tax credits and exemptions. most savings are not automatic — rather they require specific action to be taken by the estate owner.***

- **Estate Planning is a "One-Man Show."** This is certainly not true. As we enter into an era of increased specialization, most professional advisers are recognizing the need to work closely with one another in order to address properly the estate planning needs of their clients. This is particularly true the larger and/or more complex an estate becomes.

  In many instances, it becomes necessary to think in terms of putting together a competent estate planning team that will typically include an attorney, CPA, insurance adviser, trust officer, and financial consultant. Each can contribute valuable expertise to the planning process. In addition, it is vital that these professionals work together to be certain that all key documents are properly coordinated and in agreement with one another.

  Otherwise, very serious tax and nontax problems can result when, for example, one's will and/or trust and one's buy-sell documents or beneficiary designations on life insurance, annuities, or pension plans differ!

The following pages will elaborate on the material just presented and provide you with some very valuable, yet easy-to-understand information.

In Part I, the main emphasis will be placed on understanding probate, estate taxes, and other taxes that can greatly reduce your estate. However, a number of other significant concerns will be touched upon to make you aware of additional areas that need attention and planning.

Part II will provide an overview of some estate planning solutions. *Please note, however, that this information provides only an introduction to estate planning and reflects the tax law in effect at the time of printing. Specific tax, legal or insurance questions should be referred to qualified advisers.*

By the way, be sure to read the endnotes!

Part One
THE PROBLEMS

"Don't you think you guys are just a little too greedy?"

Probate

What is Probate?

Many people do not understand probate. They think it has something to do with taxes but actually, probate is the legal process by which your assets are transferred to your beneficiaries according to the provisions of your will or as determined by the state. The Probate court will supervise the distribution of assets. Some of the objectives of probate are to:

- Provide a hearing for disputes concerning the validity of wills and other documents.

- Supervise the actions of the executor of the estate.

- Inventory and appraise all assets and debts of the decedent.

- Give creditors an opportunity to collect their debts before the estate is distributed to the heirs.

- Distribute assets with clear title to the beneficiaries.

- Handle issues concerning guardianship of minor children and conservatorship of adults who are no longer mentally competent to manage themselves or their property.

How Large Must an Estate Be to Go Through Probate?

For most states, if the real estate holdings exceed $10,000/$20,000 or if the total estate, including personal effects, exceeds $30,000 to $100,000 (depending upon the state), the law requires the estate to go through probate.

- It is important to note that *there has been a lot of misunderstanding that only estates over $650,000 require* *probate.* The $650,000 is a *Federal Estate Lifetime tax exemption* and the $30,000 to $100,000 is a *State Small Estate exemption from probate.* There is no relationship between the two.

Simply Stated:	
Estates under $650,000	= no estate taxes.
Estates under ($30,000 to) $100,000	= no probate.

What Property Avoids Probate?

- **Property That Has Been Gifted To Another.**

- **Property Transferred To An Inter-Vivos Trust.**

- **Property with Beneficiary Designations such as:** Life insurance, IRAs, annuities, pension proceeds, etc.

- **Property Held in Joint Tenancy.** Joint tenancy occurs when two or more people own the same property at the same time in equal shares, with the understanding that on the death of anyone, the survivors will own the whole. Often individuals try to avoid probate by holding assets in joint tenancy. However, the use of joint tenancy has some serious potential disadvantages:

  - **Joint Tenancy does not Eliminate Probate.** Though probate is avoided at the death of the first spouse, the entire estate must go through probate upon the death of the survivor.

  - **Under Joint Tenancy, the Survivor Becomes the Sole Owner.** When one of the joint tenants dies, the surviving joint tenant then owns the entire estate. Thus, each owner MAY NOT will his or her portion of the property to a beneficiary who is not a joint owner. Therefore, a parent who is holding most or all of his or her property in joint tenancy with a new spouse may inadvertently disinherit children from a prior marriage. It is very important to remember that *joint tenancy will always take precedence over a will!*

■ **Joint Tenancy in a Community Property State Loses Full "Stepped-Up Valuation."**[2]

This can result in some large capital gains tax if the survivor later decides to sell an asset which has appreciated considerably since the original purchase.

To understand this, it is important to know that upon the death of an owner, an asset, such as a home, receives a step-up in basis . This means that the original cost basis (what the owner originally paid for the home or other asset) is revalued to the current market value.

Thus, if there is a subsequent sale of that asset, there will be no capital gains tax due. For married couples HOLDING TITLE TO THEIR PROPERTY AS COMMUNITY PROPERTY, the entire asset receives a step-up in basis at the death of the first spouse.

PROPERTY HELD IN JOINT TENANCY (*even in a community property state*), however, receives only 1/2 of the step-up in basis (the deceased owner's half), and thus, if the surviving spouse later sells the asset, capital gains tax will be due on his or her half of the asset, depending on how much the asset has appreciated since the date of the original purchase.[3] This can result in *thousands of dollars in unnecessary taxes.*

This can be particularly true where a husband and wife jointly own a privately held business because their original cost basis is often extremely low; yet if the business becomes successful, it can appreciate tremendously. If there is only a 1/2 step-up in basis, the surviving spouse could face a large capital gains tax if he or she later decides to sell the business.

Please note however, that qualified retirement plan assets, IRAs, annuities, deferred salaries, etc. do not receive a step-up at death and, thus, income taxes will be due.

- **Joint Tenancy with Children can Pose Serious Problems.** For example, legal judgments brought against an adult child can result in the assets being lost since the asset is also part of the child's estate.

- **Gifted Property Forfeits Stepped-Up Valuation.** When an individual chooses to add his or her children on as joint owners of an asset, the children not only forfeit the benefit of stepped-up valuation upon the parents' death, but they may also be subject to gift taxes and penalties.

What is the Uniform Probate Code?

In addition to the instances listed above where property avoids probate, it is important to know that a number of states have adopted what is known as a **Uniform Probate Code**. This provision offers residents of those states the opportunity to transfer certificates of deposit, savings accounts, and checking accounts under a beneficiary designation that avoids probate.

These accounts can be set up with a beneficiary designation termed *"payable on death" or* **POD**. It is important however, not to name a minor as a beneficiary. Instead name a responsible adult or a trust that divides the property according to its terms.

Additional states are considering the adoption of the **Uniform Probate Code**. Please check with a local adviser to find out if your state has adopted this provision.

What are the Costs Associated with Probate?

There are two types of fees which are allowable as part of the probate fee: **statutory fees** and **extraordinary fees.** Statutory fees are those fees that have been established by the state legislature and vary from state to state. Extraordinary fees, on the other hand, are fees that are charged by attorneys for additional services and subject to approval by the probate court.

The total fees associated with probate can vary a great deal. As mentioned previously, average costs are approximately 5% of the GROSS ESTATE, but these costs may ultimately be lower than 5% or as high as 8% to 10% or more *depending on the degree of family cooperation, the complexity of the estate, and the particular state in which the probate is conducted.*

It is important to note, too, that when it comes to probate, there can be significant differences in value between the gross and net estate.

For example:	
Gross estate:	$400,000
subtract: Loans outstanding	-$350,000
Net estate	$ 50,000

In this instance, if the individual died with an outstanding loan of $350,000, a 10% probate fee would confiscate nearly his or her entire estate ($400,000 x 10% = $40,000). Even if the probate fees were only a conservative 5% of the $400,000, that would still consume a large part of the estate ($400,000 x 5% = $20,000.)

How Long is the Probate Process?

Just as the cost of probate varies from estate to estate, the length of time it takes to probate an estate varies a great deal, as well. Some estates may complete the probate process in as early as six months, while others may take years. The same factors that influence costs will play a role in determining the length of time it takes an estate to go through probate. Again, some of these factors include: the degree of family cooperation (are there any will contests?), the complexity of the estate, and the jurisdiction in which the probate is conducted.

A long delay in settling an estate can pose many difficult and exasperating problems for heirs. For example, businesses can suffer serious disruptions. Likewise, stock portfolios and real estate holdings can incur large losses and small estates can be considerably eroded by legal fees. *Finally, heirs may have to wait a long time before they receive any money from the estate.*

Is Probate a Matter of Public Record?

Yes, a person's will is on file, along with all creditor claims and beneficiary information such as their names, addresses, and telephone numbers.

What if I Own Property in Another State or Country?

There is going to be an independent probate conducted in every state or country where you own property. Therefore, your heirs are going to have to hire a lawyer and go through the probate process in each of those states or countries!

Concerns Regarding Minor or Disabled Children

Guardianship

What Is It?

It is a legal proceeding whereby the court appoints a person or persons to act as guardians and take care of the minor or disabled children of the deceased parents. If parents do not plan properly while they are still alive, the courts will have to make decisions concerning the children without knowing the wishes of the parents.

Are there any Costs Associated with a Guardianship Hearing?

Yes, attorney fees, court filing fees, bonds, etc.

Is There any Control over the Distribution of an Estate Once a Child Reaches the Age of Majority (usually 18)?

No, when a child turns 18, he or she has the right to his or her entire portion of the estate. *Typically, this is not the best age for a child to receive a lump sum of money or an outright transfer of property.*

What Should be Taken into Consideration When Planning for a Disabled Child?

First of all, assets placed under guardianship will be considered in determining the disabled child's eligibility for SSI (Social Security Income) and Medicaid. Secondly, assets managed by a guardian will be required to be used to reimburse government agencies for services provided to the disabled child.

Common Errors That Leave the Rights of children and Other Heirs Unprotected

Not Having a Will!

Particularly if you have stepchildren, whom you have not adopted, if you die without a will or do not name them in your will, **they will be disinherited.**

Also, it is important to know that there are different consequences to dying without a will depending upon whether you live in a **separate property** state or a **community property** state.

Typically, in **separate property states**, if a married couple has one child, the surviving spouse will receive one-half of the estate and the child or his or her descendants will receive the other half. If the couple has more than one child, the surviving spouse receives one-third of the estate and the children or their descendants receive the other two-thirds of the estate. If the children are minors, the surviving spouse is subject to court supervision concerning the children's portion of the estate.

In **community property states**, however, if a married couple has children and the first spouse dies without a will, the community property will belong solely to the surviving spouse. Any separate property of the decedent, however, will be divided in the same manner as separate property in separate property states as described above.

Though the following examples are fairly typical, the **laws of intestacy** (dying without a will) vary from state to state and, therefore, it is advisable to become familiar with your own state's intestacy laws.

Failing to Keep Your Beneficiary Designations up to Date.

For example, if you fail to add the names of any additional children you may have under the beneficiary designations of your life insurance policies, annuities, IRAs etc., the children **not listed will not receive a share of the distributions.**

Having All Your Assets in Joint Tenancy with a New Spouse When You Have Children from a Prior Marriage.

If you die prior to the new spouse, the new spouse will own all of the assets regardless of what you may have specified in your will. ***Thus, your children from a prior marriage will be disinherited! Joint tenancy always takes precedence over a will!***

Failing to Name "Backup" or Contingent Beneficiaries, Guardians, and Executors.

It is essential that you designate contingent beneficiaries for your life insurance, pensions, IRAs, etc., because if your named first beneficiary predeceases you — even by a few minutes — the proceeds or distributions, that would have normally bypassed probate, will be paid to your estate rather than to your named beneficiary.

The result is that the entire proceeds will be needlessly subject to probate fees and delays (remember probate costs may be at least 5% of the gross assets — which means that at least 5% of your insurance proceeds and/or retirement plans may be unnecessarily consumed by probate fees!).

In addition, creditors will have full access to the proceeds even though most states' laws protect such proceeds from the claims of creditors when payable to named beneficiaries.

Also, it is equally important to be sure to name backup guardians, trustees and/or executors in case those you named first are unable or unwilling to assume or continue their duties.

Conservatorship

What is Conservatorship?

It is a legal proceeding by which the courts appoint someone to act as a conservator and be responsible for an individual who is no longer competent to manage himself or his property because of an illness, disability, or injury.

Is Probate for Conservatorship a Matter of Public Record?

Yes.

What are the Costs Involved in Conservatorship?

Attorney fees, court filing fees, bonds, etc.

What Else is Entailed in a Conservatorship Appointment?

The courts require the conservator to file annual reports of all financial transactions undertaken on behalf of the disabled individual. For example, a spouse named as conservator for her husband would have to give an account for what she received on her husband's behalf and what she spent. If she is elderly, inexperienced in financial matters or if the estate is complex, she would have to hire someone, such as a CPA, to do this for her.

Do Many People Have to Deal with Conservatorship Issues?

Yes, due to Alzheimer's disease and other maladies of age, the incidence of conservatorship is rising in the U.S. In addition, a serious accident may render an individual incompetent, either temporarily or permanently, at any age.

Long Term Care Concerns

What is Long Term Care?

Long Term Care refers to medical and custodial[4] services that may be required for individuals who, due to a disability, a sudden disabling illness such as a stroke or accident, or as a result of a chronic condition such as Alzheimer's disease, are limited in their ability to care for themselves and who will, as a result of their impairment, *require care over an extended period of time* (in excess of 90 days).

What are the Risks of Needing Long Term Care?

Though any of us could require long term care at any age, the risk of needing long term care services increases as we grow older. In fact, many of us will need *some type* of LTC care or assistance during our lifetimes.

A May, 1992, LTC study by *The New England Journal of Medicine* reported that about 43% of the nation's population older than 65 will be confined in a nursing home some time during their lives. This percentage

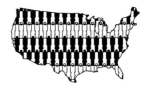

increases to 60% for those over age 85. Some people who have acute illnesses may need nursing home care for only short periods. Others, however, may need it *for many months or years*. Currently, the average stay in a nursing home is 2.5 years.

These figures do not reflect the huge number of people that are now or will eventually receive care at home!

What are the Average Costs of Long Term Care?

The costs will differ depending on a number of variables including: the level of care required; who provides the care — friends or family members, home health aids, or skilled medical personnel; whether the care provided is on a full or a part-time basis; and whether the individual receives care in his or her own home, an assisted-living facility, adult day care center, nursing home or some other facility.

Currently, nursing home costs average around $3,000 to $3,500 a month in many parts of the United States but may run as high as $5,000 a month and more in some of the eastern states! Home healthcare costs and other alternative methods of long term care can also be very expensive *and these costs are anticipated to continue to rise!*

Will My Regular Medical Coverage Cover Long Term Care?

No!

Many people are surprised to discover that while their personal medical or **Medicare coverage** may cover *some* long term-care costs, such coverage is generally approved for *only* short durations.

However, neither general insurance, nor Medicare or Medigap policies (supplemental policies that pay Medicare deductibles, co-payments, excess charges, etc.) *will cover lengthy nursing home stays or prolonged home care services!* Nor does the VA (the Veterans' Administration), in most instances, provide long-term care unless such care is required due to a service-related illness or injury.

Why Are Long-Term Care Issues Becoming Increasingly Important To Address?

As ever-increasing numbers of our population live to advanced ages, the enormous impact of long-term care needs will be felt on both a ***personal*** and a ***national level.***

On the personal level, many families are facing or will face *ONE OR MORE elder care crisis.* Not only does the disability of a loved one pose a potentially huge financial drain on family finances, but also the emotional and physical toll on everyone involved is often just as profound. The disabled loved one must endure all that is involved in a health crisis that now renders him or her dependent on either family members or professional care providers.

The family members, on the other hand, must learn quickly to juggle the myriad of new and *often emotionally taxing* responsibilities associated with their loved one's care and the demands of their own lives (marriage, career, and childrearing, etc.). To make matters worse, when an elder care crisis strikes, the potential caregiver or responsible person **often is employed and living hundreds or even thousands of miles away from the ill family member.** This, of course, only compounds the financial and emotional stress of the situation.

On the national level, burgeoning health and long-term care costs and a rapidly growing senior population have made it critical that our lawmakers take decisive steps to begin shifting the burden of long-term care costs away from government public assistance (Medicaid) and on to the private citizen. Taxpayers can no longer afford LTC for everyone, particularly in view of the fact that while fewer taxpayers are expected to enter the system, more recipients are expected to *use* the system.

Federal Estate Taxes and Other Taxes Which Affect Your Estate

What are Federal Estate Taxes?

The Federal Estate Tax is a very large transfer tax that the government levies on your right to transfer your property at your death.

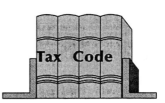

To offset these large taxes, every individual in the United States has a $211,300 tax credit (called the Unified Transfer Tax Credit) that serves to shelter up to $650,000 of assets from estate taxes and, thus, allows one to pass on up to $650,000 to the next generation tax-free. (The Taxpayer Relief Act of 1997 phases in an increase in the exemption amount to $1 million by the year 2006. Those with *qualifying family farms and businesses,* will be eligible for a $1.3 exemption, effective 12/31/97.)

However, if your estate exceeds $650,000 (or the "**applicable exclusion amount,**" depending upon the year of death), your executor of your estate will be required to file a long tax form (Form 706) with the Internal Revenue Service and the taxes *are due and payable in cash within nine months!*[5]

In most instances, federal estate taxes are not levied on a surviving spouse due to a provision in the tax code called **the unlimited marital deduction** that allows an individual to pass his or her entire estate to the surviving spouse without any federal estate taxes.

When the surviving spouse dies, however, federal estate taxes are due and heirs can face huge tax bills of 37% to 55% of an *estate's value over $650,000* (estates between $10,000,000 and $21,040,000 are assessed an additional 5%).

Those who are single, divorced or living with someone without being married will not be eligible for the **Unlimited Marital Deduction** and, thus, estate taxes will be due at their death.

FEDERAL ESTATE TAX

Taxable Estate	Tax
$ 650,000	$ 0
700,000	18,500
1,000,000	101,300
1,500,000	280,100
2,000,000	469,900
10,000,000	3,861,900

Please note in the previous chart, the $211,300 **Unified Transfer Tax Credit** (which is the equivalent of $650,000 of an estate's value) and other deductions (such as final expenses, debts, charitable deductions, etc.,) have already been taken out and, thus, it is the NET amount over $650,000 that is currently taxable at tax rates beginning at 37%.

For example, a taxable estate of $700,000 would pay a 37% tax on the AMOUNT OVER $650,000 or $18,500 ($700,000-650,000=50,000 X 37%= $18,500). The larger the estate, however, the greater percentage of tax is imposed — climbing up to 55%!

The chart below illustrates the increasing tax brackets.

MARGINAL ESTATE TAX BRACKETS

Estates Over	Top Bracket	Estates Over	Top Bracket
$650,000	37%	$1,500,000	45%
750,000	39%	2,000,000	49%
1,000,000	41%	2,500,000	53%
1,250,000	43%	Over 3,000,000	55%
Special rate on estates between$10,000,000 and $17,204,000		60%	

Needless to say, ***many heirs have faced or will face the agonizing problem of where to come up with the money to pay these estate taxes.*** Without proper planning either they would have to borrow money at hefty interest rates or worse yet, they might be forced to sell their assets, frequently at sacrifice prices. In both instances, the estate will suffer even greater losses than just the huge taxes imposed.

As mentioned previously, the Taxpayer Relief Act of 1997 raises the effective exemption amount to $1 million by the year 2006. As a result, the numbers in the marginal estate tax brackets (shown in the chart above) will change each year to reflect the increase in the Unified Transfer Tax Credit. The following chart details the annual increases.

UNIFIED TRANSFER TAX CREDIT INCREASES

Taxable Estate	Exempt Amount	Unified Credit
1998	$625,000	$202,050
1999	$650,000	$211,300
2000 and 2001	$675,000	$220,550
2002 and 2003	$700,000	$229,800
2004	$850,000	$287,300
2005	$950,000	$326,300
2006 and thereafter	$1,000,000	$345,800

What are Federal Gift Taxes?

For those who might be tempted, in their twilight years or even earlier, to give away their assets (to their children, for example) in an attempt to avoid or reduce their estate taxes, think again. There is a **federal gift tax** which levies a tax on any gifts or transfers made during one's lifetime.

This federal gift tax is "unified" with the federal estate tax and since the Tax Reform Act of 1976, the rates used for gift taxes are the same as those used for the calculation of estate taxes. Also, it is important to know that *any gifts made during your lifetime use up your $650,000 exemption and, thus, reduce the amount of the available Unified Transfer Tax Credit at death.* An exception to this would be gifts which qualify for the

annual gift tax exclusion. (See Solutions to Federal Gift Taxes.)

In addition, the gift tax is *cumulative*. This means that taxable gifts given in prior years must be taken into account in figuring the tax for the current year. The result is that *taxable gifts in prior years boost gifts in the current year into higher tax brackets, increasing tax costs significantly!*

There is yet another surprise. Gifts over the $650,000 are counted back in (at their date-of-gift value) when it comes time to value your estate.

For example, suppose you gave away $2 million in 2006, while you are alive and you die in 2007 with a $2 million remaining estate. The first $1,000,000 you give away was exempt from gift taxes, but the next $1,000,000 is taxed at estate tax rates of 37% to 45%. And your remaining $2 million estate will be taxed at rates of 49% to 55%, the rates you would pay with a $4 million estate.

The advantage of lifetime gifting, however, is that it enables you to effectively "freeze" the value of the asset you are transferring and, thus, all future appreciation of that asset will be attributed to the estate of the donee. Lifetime gifting can be a very important estate planning tool. See Solutions to Federal Gift Taxes.

Are the Rules Different for Non-Citizen Spouses?

Yes, transfers to a non-citizen spouse, both during life and at death, receive a different tax treatment. For ***lifetime transfers,*** spouses who are both U.S. citizens, can give to the other spouse any amount of property with no gift tax consequences due to a provision in the tax code known as the **gift tax marital deduction**.

As of July 14, 1988, however, only $100,000 per year can be gifted to the ***non-citizen spouse*** free of gift taxes. (Please note, we do have treaties with *some* countries that modify these general rules.)

The reason it is important to have an understanding of gift tax consequences is because gifting between spouses is occasionally used to achieve significant tax savings. For example, a spouse with a great deal of assets will sometimes transfer a portion of his or her wealth to a spouse who does not have a lot of assets in order to enable the spouse with fewer assets to make full use of important tax credits or exemptions which allow one to pass wealth tax-free to the next generation.

However some wealthy spouses, may not wish to transfer a portion of their assets to the other spouse. In these instances, life insurance on the less wealthy spouse can achieve the same desired results!

Transfers made at **death** to a non-citizen spouse (after November 10, 1988) that are over the $650,000 Unified Transfer Tax Credit require the use of a special trust known as a **Qualified Domestic Trust (QDOT)** in order to qualify for the unlimited marital deduction and, thus, defer estate taxes until the second death.

However, even with the QDOT, the estate is ultimately taxed differently than an estate in which both spouses are U.S. citizens. Transfers to a non-citizen spouse necessitate careful planning and competent legal help should be sought.

How are State Death Taxes Assessed?

State laws regarding death taxes vary a great deal. Therefore, it is important to consult with local legal counsel. In most states, though, there will be no state death tax if all but $650,000 of assets are left to or for the benefit of the surviving spouse in such a manner as to qualify for the unlimited marital deduction. However, it is important to know that *some states do not allow the unlimited marital deduction and, as a result, state death taxes will be due at the first death.*

For those owing state death taxes, federal law allows a credit **(State Death Tax Credit)** for state death taxes paid (and the amount of the credit will be deducted from federal estate tax bill), but establishes a maximum. In many states, the state death taxes can be substantially greater than the credit allowed. Therefore, the assessment of state death taxes can add significantly to your overall tax costs. Other states, on the other hand, simply `pick-up' the amount of the maximum credit as the amount of tax payable to the state and, thus, your taxes remain essentially the same as if you were only paying federal estate taxes.

Finally, some states also have what is known as an **inheritance tax system** that taxes both the heirs and the estate. Under this system, taxes are levied on the beneficiaries based on their relationship to the decedent. As a result, a surviving spouse is taxed differently than other persons receiving a distribution from the estate.

(As mentioned above, some states do not exempt from taxation transfers to the surviving spouse and others do.) Likewise, distributions to family members may receive a different tax treatment as compared to non-family members.

How are State Gift Taxes Assessed?

As with state death taxes, state gift tax laws often differ from federal laws, and many states have lower or no amounts of gifts which are excluded from gift tax. For example, the federal government has a provision in the tax code known as the **annual gift tax exclusion** that allows each individual to make gifts of $10,000 per person every year to as many people as he or she chooses free of gift taxes.

However, many states either do not have an **annual gift tax exclusion** or if they do, it excludes less than $10,000. *Therefore a gift which may be within the exclusion for federal purposes may not be within the annual exclusion for state gift tax purposes.*

Also, those who make larger gifts/transfers (over the annual exclusion amount) during their lifetime in order to make early use of the Unified Transfer Tax Credit (which shelters up to $650,000 from either federal gift or estate taxes) *may have state gift taxes to pay* depending on the state in which they reside or, in the case of gifts of real property, *the state in which the property is located.*

Lastly, some states have no marital deduction or only a partial marital deduction available for certain gifts. Therefore, any gifting programs must include an understanding of state gift tax laws!

What are Generation Skipping Taxes?

Incredible as it may seem, there is an additional and particularly harsh tax to which estate transfers may be unwittingly subjected and is known as the **Generation Skipping Transfer Tax (GSTT.)**

As of September 25, 1985, (when the laws concerning generation skipping changed) a flat tax of 55% is now imposed against any transfers made to heirs *or other persons* at least two generations below the transferor and *is assessed in addition to any other taxes owing!*

However, just as the Chinese symbol for "trouble" is also the symbol for "opportunity," so it is with generation skipping. *planning opportunities in this area present some of the most exciting wealth transfer opportunities in estate planning!* See Solutions to Generation Skipping Transfer Taxes.

Pension Tax Traps

What Types of Pensions Face Taxation?

IRAs, Keoghs, Defined Benefit, Profit Sharing, Money Purchase Pensions, Deferred Salaries or 401(k) plans, are not only subject to income taxes but may be subject to estate taxes and other taxes as well. (The Taxpayer Relief Act of 1997 introduced the Roth IRA. See page 92.)

Social Security, Veterans benefits and other government pensions, on the other hand, are not includable in one's estate for estate tax purposes but may be subject to income taxes.

What Taxes Can be Imposed on Retirement Plans at the Time Those Assets are to be Transferred to Heirs?

There are three[6] main taxes that can impact qualified pensions and IRAs:

- **Income Taxes**
- **Estate Taxes**
- **Generation Skipping Tax**

Most heirs are surprised to discover that before they can inherit qualified plan and IRA assets, not only must they pay federal and state income taxes, but also they may have to pay federal and state estate taxes.[7] Though the Taxpayer Relief act of 1997 repealed an onerous **15% excise penalty tax** that was levied against pension and IRA monies (in excess of certain IRS defined thresholds), plan assets can still be decimated by taxes.

For example, if the account balance is large or if the beneficiaries are already in a high income tax bracket, as much as 45% can be lopped off of their *inheritance just through the payment of income taxes*–and that is without figuring in any estate or generation skipping taxes that may be owed. Estate taxes, too, can claim a large portion of the plan assets. Then, if any pension monies pass to grandchildren or someone at least two generations below the donor, those assets may also be subject to generation skipping taxes. The **GST tax** is a flat 55% tax that is levied in addition to estate taxes! See *Solutions to Generation Skipping Taxes. **ALL TOLD, AS MUCH AS 70% OR MORE CAN BE LOST IN TAXES!***

When will Pension Monies be Subject to Estate Taxes?

Pension/retirement plan monies will be subject to estate taxes as soon as an individual's estate, *including the pension assets, exceeds $650,000* (or $1.25 million if a married couple have an either A-B Living Trust or a testamentary credit shelter trust). Again, the estate tax exemption threshold will increase to $1 million per person by 2006.

Is It Possible for Heirs to Continue the Income Tax Deferral on Inherited Plans?

It is extremely important to know that *with proper planning,* many plan participants and/ or IRA owners can set it up for their heirs to be able to receive distributions from their inherited plans over a period of years or even over their lifetime. ***In many instances, this can save thousands of dollars of taxes and allow for decades of income tax deferral and compound growth!***

On the other hand, if as a result of poor planning, the beneficiary must receive the proceeds in a lump sum in the year following the owner's death, he or she must report as ordinary income *the entire account balance* on his or her income tax return. This, in many instances, will place the beneficiary in the highest federal and state income tax bracket. Thus, as mentioned above, as much as 45% of the beneficiary's inheritance can be lost to just to income taxes.

In order to enable heirs to take advantage of valuable income tax deferral opportunities, it is essential that plan participants/IRA owners consult with qualified financial planning or legal professionals *regarding important rules that must be followed and key decisions that must be made irrevocably prior to age 70 ½* (the age–with limited exceptions–at which mandatory distributions from one's retirement plans and IRAs are required)!

Why is Liquidity Planning is Essential for Income and Estate Tax Planning?

Many plans are not able to continue the income tax deferral once they are inherited because the executor needs to take a lump sum in order to pay estate taxes. ***"All the great planning in the world" won't protect plan beneficiaries who don't have the money to pay any estate taxes owing.*** Failure to provide an alternative source of liquidity to pay estate and possible generation skipping taxes can ruin the best-laid plans for income tax deferral!

Also, many people mistakenly assume that they will have plenty of money to pay estate taxes by simply taking the money from their qualified plans or IRAs. Often, they have over estimated the resources that they will have available because they have failed to take the income tax liability on plan assets into consideration.

An excellent alternative to taking money out of the plan to pay estate taxes (which then *also* creates an immediate income tax liability), is to purchase second-to-die life insurance for couples and single life policies for those who are unmarried. Be sure to have the insurance owned by either an irrevocable life insurance trust or an adult beneficiary in order to keep the insurance proceeds out of the owner's estate. (See *Solutions to Pension Tax Traps.*)

Business Continuation Concerns

Businessowners, in particular, need to make business succession and estate planning a top priority. Those who are unplanned, or who have failed to plan properly, are leaving their businesses, themselves, their families, their employees, and in some instances, other businesses with whom they work, extremely vulnerable. The failure to plan and make certain that those plans are set up correctly and kept current can have serious consequences.

What Are Some of the Risks that May Result From Failure to Plan Properly?

- Severe Financial Strain or Loss

- Disruption, Forced Sale or Liquidation of the Business

- Unexpected Tax Traps

- Disputes Between Surviving Businessowners and Heirs;

- Family Conflicts.

Let's Look at Each One of These Potential Threats More Carefully:

Severe Financial Strain Or Loss

The death or disability of a key businessowner or employee can result in a severe financial strain or loss to the business and to the family members of the deceased or disabled owner.

Works in progress, pending negotiations, sales promotions and other important projects can be seriously impacted. Often, the roles and expertise of the co-owners of the business vary a great deal and are not readily interchangeable. For example, one businessowner may have expert knowledge with regard to financial or technical matters while another co-owner may be the sales and marketing whiz of the company.

At the sudden death or disability of a key owner or employee, the company may be unable to find a suitable replacement or it may have to incur a great deal of additional expense in order to find, recruit, train, *and pay the salary* of the new replacement. During this same time, the company or the surviving co-owners also may be encumbered by an obligation to buy back the decedent's share of the business.

If the company is already straddled with debt, the death or disability of a key businessowner or employee will only serve to *strike an additional blow.* If more than one key owner or employee is killed in a common accident or if another key owner or employee dies or becomes disabled during the next few years, the repercussions could be devastating.

Finally, it is important to point out that the family of the deceased or disabled owner *(as well as the families of the surviving owners)* may be left vulnerable and dependent upon the continued success of the business. In the case of a sole **proprietorship** or a sole-owner corporation, the business may die with the businessowner. *The family, however, could be left with the debts, final expenses, probate fees, estate taxes, etc.*

Disruption, Forced Sale or Liquidation of a Business

As discussed above, the death, disability (or other departure) of a key businessowner or employee can cause serious disruptions in business activities. Ultimately, the company may not be able to recover or fill the void that occurs from the loss of such a key individual and the company will be forced to sell or liquidate.

Unexpected Tax Traps

Designing a proper business succession and estate plan requires expert tax, legal, and insurance advice. This is not an area to try "do-it-yourself" planning. The reason is that there are many potential tax traps. Below are only a few of the potential traps of which you need to be aware and discuss with knowledgeable advisers:

- **Out-of date or UNCOORDINATED wills, trusts, buy-sell agreements, etc.,** can cause some highly "unpleasant" tax (and non-tax) surprises.

- **Family attribution rules:** If you own an incorporated family business (a C corporation or an S Corporation with C corporation **accumulated earnings and profits**), it is essential that you review very carefully your business succession plans. A buy-out that is executed incorrectly may trigger the complex tax laws associated with incorporated family-owned businesses. As a result, you may incur a *MUCH larger income-tax liability on the sale of your business!*

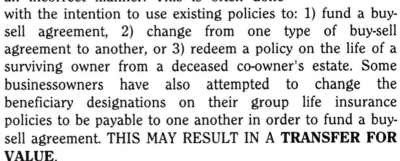

- **Transfer for value rules:** Often businessowners will mistakenly transfer or sell one or more life insurance policies in an incorrect manner. This is often done with the intention to use existing policies to: 1) fund a buy-sell agreement, 2) change from one type of buy-sell agreement to another, or 3) redeem a policy on the life of a surviving owner from a deceased co-owner's estate. Some businessowners have also attempted to change the beneficiary designations on their group life insurance policies to be payable to one another in order to fund a buy-sell agreement. THIS MAY RESULT IN A **TRANSFER FOR VALUE**.

  An incorrect transfer, sale or exchange of a beneficial interest in a life insurance policy can cause the death benefit to lose its income-tax-free status and *result in the payment of thousands of dollars of unnecessary income taxes!*

- **The incorrect type of business succession plan or buy-sell agreement for your business** (See solutions to Business Transfer Traps). There are different types of buy-out arrangements and buy-sell agreements. Each has different tax consequences and offers various advantages and disadvantages depending upon your individual circumstances, and the type of business you own (sole proprietor, partnership, C Corporation, S Corporation, limited partnership, limited liability company, professional partnership or corporation, etc.), and whether at least 51% of your business is family owned.

It is important to know that changes from one type of buy-sell agreement to another should be reviewed carefully *to avoid potential tax traps.*

Also, *changes from one form of business ownership to another* (for example, from a S corporation to a C corporation or from a partnership to a C corporation, etc.,) will necessitate a careful review of ALL PRIOR BUY-SELL PLANNING TO MAKE ABSOLUTELY CERTAIN THAT YOUR BUSINESS SUCCESSION PLANS ARE SET UP CORRECTLY FOR YOUR NEW FORM OF BUSINESS!

Disputes Between the Surviving Businessowners and Heirs.

Without proper planning, you may wind up in business with your deceased co-owner's spouse (and his or her new spouse) or children. Of course, some businessowners have harmonious relationships with the family members of their associates. In fact, some family members already may be employed in the business or informal plans may have been made to have one or more heirs enter the business at a later date.

In other situations, however, grievous conflicts may arise between the surviving owners and the heirs. Often, the needs of the heirs and the surviving businessowners can be diametrically opposed. Serious disputes may arise over money, job positions, business decisions, employee benefits, salary increases and bonuses for the surviving owners, expansion plans, etc.

Family Conflicts.

Do you plan on having any of your children enter your business? How old are they currently? How do the various family members get along with one another? Will family members who are not active in the business but who have inherited partial ownership interfere with those family members who are active in the business?

On the other hand, will the inactive family members be treated fairly? Can the family members not active in the business be compensated with life insurance or other assets from the estate? ***These and other similar questions are important to take into consideration if family conflicts are to be kept to a minimum.***

What is Included in Your Estate?

Virtually everything you own or have an incidence of ownership in, including life insurance on yourself and your retirement account monies, is included in your estate even though the proceeds are payable to a named beneficiary!

An estate includes all of an individual's property including:

• Real Estate at Market Value	• Cash
• Personal Property (jewelry, art, automobiles, home furnishings, etc.)	• Stocks and Bonds. Life insurance, Pensions, Retirement Accounts, and Deferred Salaries
• Business Interests	• Uncollected Personal Loans

Most people are surprised to learn that the life insurance they own on their own lives, though immune to income taxes, is included in their estate for estate tax purposes. This can be very significant in that not only will the insurance inflate the size of the estate, but also up to 55% of the insurance proceeds could be paid out in estate taxes (depending on the size of their estate).

For example, many individuals have anywhere from $100,000 to $500,000 in life insurance. $500,000 of life insurance in an estate tax bracket of 40% would result in $200,000 in taxes! There are planning techniques available to keep life insurance proceeds excluded from the estate, thus resulting in thousands of dollars of tax savings.

In addition, it is important to note, as mentioned in the section on Pension Tax Traps, that pensions, retirement accounts and deferred salaries are *frequently overlooked in estate planning because retirees don't realize these assets are subject to estate taxes.*

Finally, many people, unaware of how high a business interest can be valued, can be in for a real shock. At death, a business must be valued by techniques acceptable to the IRS. *Therefore, if you own a company that earns $100,000 a year, that company may ultimately be valued at $1 million and included in your estate!*

Who Should Consider Estate Planning?

Estate planning is NOT just for the wealthy! Due to the rapid increase in real estate values over the past 20 years, as well as the inclusion of qualified retirement plans and life insurance into the estate for estate tax purposes, **many middle income families will be hit hard by taxes and other expenses such as those associated with probate**. The sad fact is that it is the smaller estates that can least afford such expenses.

In addition, it is extremely important to realize that an "estate" that does not appear to have an estate tax problem now may have one later. Many estates, particularly those with real estate, investments, or business interests, may double, triple or even quadruple in just a few short years. The result is that as the estate grows, the severity of the tax bite increases significantly!

Therefore, it is highly advantageous to begin estate planning as early as possible. The sooner one starts, the more opportunities there are available to minimize and reduce estate taxes.

Are There People who have Failed to Plan Properly for Their Estate? What has been the Result?

The shocking truth is that the probate records through the years have been filled with the names of celebrities and other very successful and prominent people who suffered huge losses to their estates. *One would have thought that these individuals would have had available to them the very best advisers. Unfortunately, however, something went wrong* for either they were not advised properly and, thus, did not realize the severe consequences their estates would suffer by failing to do estate planning or they procrastinated until it was too late.

The following are just a few of the many well-known individuals listed in the public probate records whose estates sustained major losses:

NAME	VALUE OF THE ESTATE	WHAT THE IRS and OTHERS RECEIVED	WHAT THE HEIRS RECEIVED	PERCENT OF SHRINKAGE
Marilyn Monroe	$ 819,176	$ 448,750	$ 370,426	55%
Henry J. Kaiser, Sr.	5,597,772	2,488,364	3,109,408	44%
William Holden	6,064,731	4,083,853	1,980,878	67%
Elvis Presley	10,165,434	7,374,635	2,790,799	73%
Alwin C. Ernst, CPA	12,642,431	7,124,112	5,518,319	56%
J.P. Morgan	17,121,482	11,893,691	5,227,791	69%
William E. Boeing	22,386,158	10,589,748	11,796,410	47%
J.D. Rockefeller, Sr.	26,905,182	17,124,988	9,780,194	64%
Frederick Vanderbilt	76,838,530	42,846,112	33,992,418	56%

How Large is Your Estate?

List your assets and subtract your liabilities to help determine your net estate.

Assets	In Your Name	In Your Spouse's	Jointly Owned
Personal residence	$	$	$
Other real estate			
Personal property			
(jewelry, cars, furnishings, etc.)			
Checking/savings accounts			
Certificates of Deposit (CDs)			
Annuities			
Stocks and Bonds			
Mutual Funds			
Limited Partnerships			
Collectibles (stamps, coins, art)			
IRA's			
Pension or profit sharing plans			
Life insurance (owned outright)			
Business Interests			
Total Assets	$	$	$
Liabilities			
Mortgages	$	$	$
Other loans or debts			
Total Liabilities	$	$	$
Net Estate	$	$	$

How Quickly Can Your Estate Double?

To determine how quickly your estate (or a particular asset) will double in value if it grows by a certain percentage each year, divide the number 72 by the anticipated rate of growth:

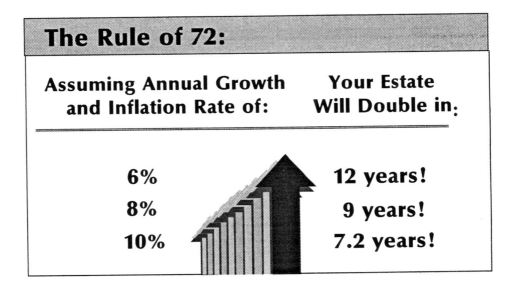

The Rule of 72:

Assuming Annual Growth and Inflation Rate of:	Your Estate Will Double in:
6%	12 years!
8%	9 years!
10%	7.2 years!

Part Two

THE SOLUTIONS

*"Hi. I'm the bluebird of inside but commonly
misunderstood information."*

Solution to Probate

The Living Trust

What is a Living Trust?

A living trust,[8] simply stated, is a trust created during your lifetime which provides for the distribution of assets that are in the trust at your death. During your lifetime, you retain the right to revoke (cancel) the trust, change its terms, or regain possession of the property in the trust.

How does the Living Trust Avoid Probate?

Probate court can only exercise authority over property owned by an individual at his or her death. Once you transfer the property to the trust, you do not own it as an individual but rather own and manage it as a trustee (however, you have complete control over your assets.)

Also, because there has been a lifetime transfer of the property to the trust, and the trust provides what is to be done with the property on your death, there would be no need for the probate court to be involved in the transfer of those assets at death[9].

It is important to remember, though, that *only those assets which are transferred to the trust avoid probate*. A **pour-over will** is usually included with a living trust and it gives instructions for the disposition of assets not put in the trust. However, assets transferred after death to the trust with the **pour-over will** are not protected from probate.

The Living Trust Avoids Probate and Thus, You Have:
• No Court Hearings   • No Public Record • No Executor Fees   • No Time Delays • No Bond Premiums

How Can a Living Trust Solve Problems Associated with Joint Tenancy?

Since having one's assets in trust avoids probate, there is no need to add children on as joint tenants to your assets. Thus, you avoid the dangers associated with having the children as joint tenants as well as the loss in the full step-up in value of those assets at your death.

Spouses who live in a COMMUNITY PROPERTY state (even temporarily) may create a living trust which *takes advantage of the community property benefit of a full step-up in basis at the death of the first spouse.* Thereafter, even if they move to another state, their assets in trust will have the advantage of community property status.

In addition to the full step-up in basis, assets held in community property do not automatically become the sole property of the survivor as is the case of joint tenancy. Rather, each spouse is considered to own 1/2 of the property, and at death, can will his or her half to chosen beneficiaries. However, if the first spouse-to-die dies without a will, the property will belong solely to the surviving spouse.

In a living trust, of course, this would not occur because a living trust includes a will and provides instructions as to what your wishes are in regard to the disposition of your property.

For those living in separate property states, it is important to get advice from either a knowledgeable real estate agent or lawyer as to the best way to hold title to your property for your particular circumstances and wishes.

Solutions to the Concerns for Minor or Disabled Children

A Will, a Living Trust, and Life Insurance

How does a Will and Living Trust avoid Guardianship Problems?

A will is certainly the most basic estate planning tool necessary in providing for the care of minor children. However, a will does have some limitations. A will does not avoid probate or a guardianship hearing[10] and it cannot manage the assets or plan for the proper distributions of those assets to the children at appropriate ages.

Therefore, If you were to die without a living trust, the court would be required to set up a trust to hold the assets until the minor children become adults (usually age 18) or to provide for the continuing care of handicapped children of any age. The trust would be very restrictive and the trustee would be required to report regularly to the court. As with all probate proceedings, there are court costs, attorney fees, etc., and all *too often small estates are greatly reduced by such administrative fees.*

If, on the other hand, you have a will and a living trust, you can name a guardian/trustee *of your choice* to be responsible for your children and you can state how you want your funds used in the raising of your children. Please note that it is possible to name one individual (or couple) to act as a guardian and another to act as trustee of the child's financial assets, such as a bank trustee or a trusted individual who is experienced in the management of money.

In addition, the trustee you select can:

- Pay for your children's health, support and education

- Invest assets on behalf of your children,

- Provide for the individual needs of each child, and

- Distribute assets to children at ages selected by parents.

Are There Special Planning Provisions Which Can be Included in a Living Trust Which Will Protect the Interests of a Disabled Child or Other Disabled Heir?

Yes, a living trust can be designed to meet the changing needs of the disabled child (or other disabled heir) over his or her lifetime. The document can be drafted in such a way as to both preserve eligibility for need based government programs and insulate the trust assets from government claims for reimbursement. The family may set up a separate trust for the disabled child or include these special provisions in a trust which also provides for other family members.

How Does Life Insurance Protect the Children's Future?

Life insurance on the lives of the parents can furnish inexpensively *and guarantee* that there *will be funds available* to provide for the children's needs (including college funding) even if one or both parents dies *at any time* while the children are still minors. In addition, should both parents die before their children are grown, life insurance would ease the financial responsibility placed on the guardians who may have children of their own to support or who, as in the case of grandparents, may be retired and living on a fixed income.

In addition, life insurance can be a "**great equalizer**." Many situations arise where it is difficult to make fair and equitable distributions to various family members such as:

- Married persons who have children from a prior marriage who want to provide for their present spouse and any children from that marriage as well as their children from a prior marriage in a fair manner.

- Those who have more than one child but are planning to transfer a large asset, such as a business, to only one of their children because that particular child wants to work in the business and the others do not.

Life insurance creates the funds, and at a discount, to make it possible to have equitable distributions!

Solutions to Conservatorship

What Important Documents are Necessary to Protect an Individual who Becomes Disabled or Incapacitated?

These documents either may be drafted separately or included with a living trust..

A Durable Power of Attorney.

It is a legal document that gives the right, which can be broad or very limited, to act legally for someone. If the power is a "durable" power of attorney (and not just a general power of attorney), the right to act continues even if the person giving the power becomes legally incompetent. Thus, the durable power of attorney allows you to choose, while you are still competent, whom is to act for you should you become incompetent. If you have a living trust, the Durable Power of Attorney is only needed for assets still remaining outside the trust (the **successor trustee**, who may also have the durable power of attorney, is the one who manages the assets within the trust).

A Durable Power of Attorney for Health Care.

A Durable Power of Attorney for Health Care is designed to allow you to specify whom you would want to make binding health care decisions for you in case you became unable to do so yourself.

A Living Will.

A living will has been called a "die with dignity will." This document allows you to state that you do not wish your life to be prolonged by artificial means once it has been determined that there is no reasonable expectation of recovery.

Appointment of Conservator.

An Appointment of Conservator document allows you to designate a legal guardian to be responsible for your person if you become incompetent.

Solutions to Long Term Care Concerns

Planning ahead for long term care needs **before a crisis strikes** protects *you, your assets*, and *your heirs*. However, for some individuals, there may be relatively little time to plan because the problem may already be at hand. Therefore, it is important to know what possible solutions may exist under either condition.

What Options are Available to Fund Long Term Care Costs?

Today, there remains basically three options available for funding long term care needs:

- Cash

- Medicaid

- Long Term Care Insurance

Cash

With annual nursing home costs ranging from $30,000 to $60,000 **or more**, and other long term care services provided outside a nursing home also potentially very expensive, family resources can be consumed quickly *when only one spouse becomes ill.* Very few families can sustain the crushing impact of long term care costs if the second spouse subsequently becomes ill.

Medicaid (known as Medi-Cal in California)

Medicaid is a form of welfare that picks up long-term care costs only if the ill person's income is insufficient to pay for nursing home costs and he or she no longer has other means to pay for  long term care. In order to qualify for Medicaid assistance, the ill person (and his or her spouse, if married) must "**spend down**" their assets, to certain federal and state prescribed limits. Because the federal government allows each state a certain amount of flexibility in applying the law, state laws vary to a certain extent on how much income and assets are allowed to be kept when one becomes eligible for Medicaid. (Check your state's requirements.)

Spend down requirements will also differ depending on whether the Medicaid applicant is single or married. It is extremely important that married couples become alert to the fact that, with the exception of *income received in the name of the spouse not entering a nursing home*, all other assets of both spouses, including assets protected by prenuptial agreements and/or separate property agreements, *are considered joint assets and are countable under Medicaid law!* This is a particularly important consideration for those who enter second marriages later in life!

In recent years, Medicaid eligibility requirements have become increasingly strict and some planning opportunities are no longer allowed. In fact, if you or a family member have done any planning involving Medicaid trusts, it is vital to have the trust documents reviewed by a attorney who is knowledgeable in the area of elder law. On June 1, 1986 congress passed a law that *retroactively banned* the use of some trusts that were set up to protect assets from Medicaid. Then again, on August 11, 1993, Congress passed another law that further restricted the use of certain trusts for Medicaid planning purposes.

However, there are still some viable planning opportunities that can help you protect family assets in the event that either you or a loved one must enter a nursing home. A *brief* description follows of three main planning strategies that are used today.

(*UPDATE:* Please note that in August of 1996 Congress passed another bill that goes into effect January 1, 1997. This bill amends Medicaid law. Advisers are not quite certain as to the full ramifications of this new addition to the law. Please consult with attorneys who work with the Medicaid system and nursing homes. The strategies listed below may be impacted by the new bill.)

1. Converting Non-Exempt Assets Into Exempt Assets.

The first strategy is to "spend" assets that Medicaid considers *countable* on assets that are *exempt* from Medicaid. It is important to know, therefore, that assets are divided for purposes of Medicaid qualification into:

- **Exempt Assets (non-countable assets):** Your primary residence[11], a car, an amount of cash (usually $2,000), personal jewelry, household items, a burial plot, term life insurance, business property (check your state) and a few other nominal assets.

- **Non-Exempt Assets (countable assets):** Everything else you (and your spouse) own!

- **Inaccessible Assets:** Non-exempt assets that have been made unavailable to Medicaid (usually by gifting or transferring the assets to an irrevocable trust).

Medicaid allows you to spend **NON-EXEMPT ASSETS (countable assets)** at any time to:

- **Purchase Exempt Assets** (for example, to upgrade a family car or purchase household furnishings),

- **Pay For Certain Services** such as car or household repairs, or

- **Pay Debts** including the home mortgage.

In some instances, it also may be advisable for couples where one spouse must enter a nursing home, to consider using NON-EXEMPT ASSETS to purchase, *in the at-home spouse's name alone,* an **immediate annuity** (which pays an immediate income). Under Medicaid rules, the at-home spouse is allowed to keep all his or her own income. *NOT ALL STATES ALLOW THIS AS A METHOD TO PROTECT ASSETS FROM MEDICAID.* Check your state's *current* laws.

2. Gifting Cash or Other Assets.

The second strategy involves gifting *non-exempt* assets out of your estate. However, gifting non-exempt assets (countable assets) and, in some cases your primary residence, will trigger a period of Medicaid ineligibility. The period of ineligibility, as of August 11, 1993, will be determined by:

- The **look-back period** (see below) and

- The value of the asset divided by the average monthly nursing home cost in your area.

To understand the rules regarding the *period of ineligibility* it is important to know that from the date you first apply for Medicaid assistance *or first enter a nursing home* (if you had to **spend down** in order to qualify for Medicaid),

Medicaid has the right to "look back" at your finances for a period of months. Until recently, that look-back period was 30 months. But as of August 11, 1993, the period has been extended to 36 months for *outright transfers* to another person and 60 months for transfers made to or from *certain types of trusts.*

Therefore, if you transfer non-exempt assets, for less than fair market value WITHIN the look-back period (within 36 or 60 months of applying for Medicaid or entering a nursing home), Medicaid declares you ineligible for a period of time. Many people mistakenly believe that the look-back period is the number of months that you are disqualified from receiving Medicaid benefits. This is untrue.

To determine the actual period of ineligibility (the number of months that you would be ineligible for Medicaid), you would divide the value of the asset transferred by the average monthly nursing home bill as established by your state's welfare department.

For example, if you transferred $15,000 in cash or other assets WITHIN the look-back period, and your state's average monthly nursing home bill were $3,000, you would be ineligible for Medicaid benefits for 5 months after the transfer of assets (15 divided by 3 = 5).

However, if you were, instead, to make a much larger transfer of cash or other assets and then apply for Medicaid any time within the **look-back period**, *your actual period of ineligibility could be much longer than 36 months* (or 60 months for transfers made to or from a trust)! For example, if you transferred $210,000 WITHIN the look-back period, your period of Medicaid ineligibility would be 70 months (210,000 divided by 3,000 = 70)!

On the other hand, if you transferred ANY AMOUNT prior to the look-back period (more than 36 or 60 months before applying for Medicaid benefits), there would be no period of ineligibility as a result of the transfer.

3. Transferring Assets to Special Trusts.

The third strategy involves the use of special trusts:

- An **income only trust** or

- A **special needs trust** (a trust set up for a disabled family member).

    Check with an attorney knowledgeable in elder law.

The paragraphs above provide only a *brief summation* of some of the Medicaid rules. *It is essential, therefore, that you seek expert counsel with regard to Medicaid Planning.*

Long Term Care Insurance

Long term care insurance, as you might guess, is designed to pay the costs associated with long term care. Assuming you are healthy enough to qualify and can comfortably afford to pay the premium, a **LTC** policy can help protect your estate entirely *or,* if you choose a smaller benefit package (see below), *it can at least allow you to coordinate the LTC insurance with Medicaid planning.*

In an effort to accommodate people's different needs and pocketbooks, insurance companies offer policyholders a variety of options including the choice of:

- **A daily benefit** usually ranging between $50 and $250 a day.

- **A benefit period** (how long the benefit will last)–one, two, three, 5, 10 years etc., or for life.

- **An elimination period** (the number of days you self pay before the policy begins to pay) - from zero days to 365 days.

- **Optional inflation rider** increases **daily benefit** amount annually by a certain percentage in order to allow benefits to keep up with inflation.

- **Guaranteed purchase option** can be an alternative to the optional inflation rider (above). It allows policyholder to add benefits to the policy every 1-3 years to keep pace with inflation *without evidence of insurability.*

It is important to know that some policies pay only for care in nursing homes, while other policies pay only for care at home. Still others pay for both nursing home and home care. In addition, some policies also cover services provided in adult day care centers and other community facilities.

Many insurance companies will also allow you to buy long-term care benefits as part of an individual life insurance policy. Under this arrangement, a certain percentage of the policy's death benefit is paid when the policyholder requires long-term care. However, the death benefit and the cash values are reduced by the amount of long-term care benefits paid.

Another alternative, available only in a few states that have been able to participate in what is known as the Robert Wood Johnson Foundation Partnership Plans, are state-certified Long-term care "partnership" policies. Such policies provide policyowners asset protection from Medicaid spend-down for later some or a majority of their assets even if the policyowner requires additional nursing home care after the policy benefits have been exhausted. (Check with your state.)

A final note! In comparing policies, it is essential to also be alert to what are known as the **benefit triggers.** The benefit triggers are used to define when benefits are paid. Most policies today have similar benefit trigger definitions.

However, it is important to be aware of the fact that many LTC policies issued up to 1989 contained benefit triggers that often MADE IT DIFFICULT TO QUALIFY FOR BENEFITS. Since that time, the National Association of Insurance Commissioners (NAIC) has developed model regulation establishing minimum standards for long-term care policies.

If you have an older policy, it is extremely important that you have the policy reviewed by an insurance agent who is knowledgeable with regard to long-term care policies!

TAX UPDATE: As a result of the enactment in 1996 of the Health Insurance Portability and Accountability Act (HIPPA), also known as the Kennedy-Kassenbaum Bill, long-term care insurance may now either be: "qualified" or "non-qualified." Qualified policies, also known as tax qualified policies, must meet certain federal requirements and are eligible for limited tax deductions tax deductions based on one's age at the end of the tax year the policy was issued,

In order to take advantage of the tax deductions, however, taxpayers must itemize their deductions on their tax returns and the cost of their long-term care insurance premiums along with other qualifying medical expenses must exceed 7.5% of their adjusted gross income. Then, *only* the portion of their medical expenses that *exceeds the 7.5%* threshold can be deducted. Non-qualified policies are not eligible for any tax deductions. (The exception to this is that *group long-term policies* paid by an employer are deductible as a business expense and are not subject to the 7.5% floor.)

What is surprising is that tax-qualified policies currently have fewer and more restrictive benefit triggers than non-qualified policies. Therefore, it may be more difficult for insureds covered under tax qualified policies to qualify for benefits. "Non-qualified" policies issued before January 1, 1997, however, are grandfathered and are eligible for the same tax deductions as the tax-qualified plans as long as there have been no material changes made to the policy. Therefore, it may be important not to replace a policy that was issued before January 1, 1997 without a thorough comparison. Please consult with a qualified insurance agent or financial planner.

Solutions to Federal Estate Taxes

There are many ways, including some which may not be as well known, to reduce estate taxes. Here are five of the more common methods:

A-B Living Trust

Many people are unaware of the tremendous estate tax savings they can achieve by using an A-B living trust (also known as a credit shelter or bypass trust) . This legal instrument allows a married couple to shelter up to $1.25 million from estate taxes and thus, save up to $330,000 off their taxes *(or more depending on the year of death of each spouse)*. The same estate tax savings can be achieved with a properly drafted will that provides for the creation of a bypass trust at death. However, a probate proceeding would be required if a will instead of a living trust is used.

How is This Done?

Each individual in the United States has a $211,300 tax credit (called a **Unified Transfer Credit)** on his estate taxes, allowing him to leave $650,000 to the next generation tax-free. *If the $650,000 is left to the surviving spouse instead of to the next generation the $211,300 estate tax credit is wasted.*

This is where the A-B living trust comes in. Instead of leaving everything outright to the surviving spouse, a married couple can create an A-B trust which preserves the Unified Transfer Tax Credit of both spouses. The way it works is the trust, created while both are alive, is split into two trusts, A and B, after the death of the first spouse.

At this time, an amount equal to the Unified Transfer Tax Credit (currently $650,000) would be selected to go into the decedent's B trust. (For larger estates, a decision may be made to place more that $650,000 into the decedent's trust and pay some of the estate taxes at the first death in order to insulate all future growth of those assets from estate taxes.) The balance of the estate would pass to the survivor's A trust. The B trust then becomes irrevocable, and thus, is considered to be out of the spouse's estate.

Meanwhile, the survivor is entitled to income from both A and B, and may even use the principal of B for healthcare, education, maintenance or support if needed. Upon the death of the survivor, both trusts pass to the couple's heirs.

For example, assume a $1.25 million estate:

The A - B Trust			
SURVIVOR'S A TRUST:	$650,000*	DECEDENT'S B TRUST:	$650,000**
Estate Tax	$211,300	Estate Tax	$211,300
Unified Credit	− 211,300	Unified Credit	−211,300
Estate Tax Due	-0-	Estate Tax Due	-0-
*Assumes no growth in survivor's estate. Amounts over $650,000 would be subject to estate taxes.		**All future growth is insulated from estate taxes in both spouses' estates!	

Is There a Way to Guarantee That Assets Left to My Current Spouse Above the $650,000 Unified Credit Threshold Will Ultimately Pass to Heirs of My Choosing such as to Children From a Prior and/or Present Marriage and Others and Not to the Survivor's Heirs or New Spouse?

Yes. For individuals who are married and whose share of the marital assets (or their own separate property) is over $650,000, an A-B-C trust system can be used. The "C" part of the trust is known as a **Qualified Terminable Interest Property (QTIP) Trust**. Assets over the $650,000 Unified Credit amount are placed in this trust and qualify for the unlimited marital deduction and, thus, no estate taxes will be due upon the first death. The surviving spouse must receive all the *income* from the trust each year for life. At the surviving spouse's death, however, *the remaining principal is taxed in his or her estate* and what's left after the estate taxes are paid is then transferred to the chosen beneficiaries of the first *spouse to die.*

Lifetime Gifts

Each year every person is allowed to give up to $10,000 per person (married couples can gift $20,000) to as many people as he or she wishes, free of federal gift or estate taxes. (The Taxpayer Relief Act of 1997 indexes the exclusion amount for inflation but only in $1,000 increments and rounded down. For example, if the indexed amount is $10,999, the donor will still only get a $10,00 exclusion that year.)

This tax provision is called the **annual gift tax exclusion.**[12] Therefore, a person (or a couple) with a large estate, for example, could begin to pare it down by giving $10,000 (or $20,000 per couple) to their children, their children's spouses, grandchildren or others each year. As a result, over time, they could reduce the size of their taxable estate considerably, and at the same time, transfer money safely to heirs which otherwise would have been lost to taxes. The sample chart below demonstrates the power of the **annual gift tax exclusion:**

Annual Gift	Number of Years Annual Gifts Are Made		
	5 yrs	**10 yrs**	**20 yrs**
$10,000	$63,348*	$156,459	$494,227
$20,000	126,715	312,906	988,456
$30,000	190,076	469,363	1,482,687
$40,000	253,434	625,811	1,976,920
$100,000	633,595	1,564,546	4,942,292

Assumes gifted assets continue to grow at 8% per year after the gift is made (the new rules regarding indexing are not figured into these calculations).

Also, there are many instances when larger lifetime gifts (those over the $10,000 **annual exclusion** amount or even over the $625,000 Unified Credit amount) should be considered. This is particularly true if one has assets that are expected to appreciate a great deal. On the other hand, it may be wiser to retain assets which *have already greatly appreciated* in order for the heirs to receive a step-up in basis at the owner's death. Remember that gifted property (with the exception of life insurance) does not receive a step-up in basis, and, thus, the donee receives the donor's basis in the property (with some credit given for any gift or generation skipping taxes paid).

However, It should be noted, that under the Taxpayer Relief Act of 1997, the new capital gains provision which allows a $250,000 ($500,000 if married and filing jointly) capital gains exclusion from for the sale of a principal residence (that has been owner occupied for at least two of the last five years) may provide an important planning opportunity for some estate owners who are considering gifting a residence to an heir.

Important — If some of the annual gift amount is used to purchase life insurance outside of the estate, ***the potential wealth building effect becomes dramatic!***

Tax-Favored Insurance Product — The 1% Solution!

Tax-favored life insurance products are rapidly gaining popularity. These policies don't actually reduce estate taxes, ***they help pay them.***

Using the *income tax free,* "discounted dollars" from life insurance to pay estate taxes and provide for other financial needs is not a new idea, but considering how well these insurance products work and the ***enormous amount of money they save by inexpensively providing the liquidity to pay estate taxes,*** it is still surprising how many people are unaware of the tremendous advantages of insurance planning. Savvy advisers, however, have *for years* been recommending and implementing insurance in their planning to achieve cost-effective solutions for their clients.

THE LEVERAGE OF LIFE INSURANCE

Premiums Paid On	Ages	Annual Premiums	Total Premiums
$250,000 Police (Second-to-Die) for approximately 10 years	50/50	$2,000	$20,000
	60/60	3,000	30,000
	70/70	6,000	60,000
$500,000 Policy (Second-to-Die) for approximately 10 years	50/50	$4,000	$40,000
	60/60	6,000	60,000
	70/70	12,000	120,000

Life Insurance costs will vary depending upon the amount of insurance purchased, the type of policy selected (single or joint life policies, term, whole life, universal life, variable life, etc.) and the age, sex, health, and lifestyle (smoker/non-smoker, hazardous vocations or hobbies, etc.) of the proposed insured.

There are many types of policies available — each designed to meet specific planning needs and to offer varied features and benefits. Two common policies, for example, used in estate planning are:

1. **Joint first-to-die** policies

   - Covers two or more lives

   - Pays at the first death

2. **Second-to-die** policies

   - Covers two lives

   - Pays only at the second death (for example, when estate taxes are due on a couple's estate).

Joint first- and second-to-die policies are cheaper than single life policies. However, there are many instances where single life policies are selected or a combination of both types of policies are used to accomplish specific planning objectives.

This is true particularly in those instances where there is a need for either **income** or **liquidity** at the first death or for those individuals who wish to accumulate large cash values in their policies to be used for lifetime purposes.

Often **income** is needed after the first death to provide ongoing financial support for the surviving spouse, children, and others who may have been dependent on the decedent for financial assistance. *Many times there is a substantial need for income replacement due to the loss of the income of the first spouse-to-die or the drop in Social Security, Veterans, or pension benefits due to the discontinuance of the decedent's portion of the benefits.*

Liquidity Needs Usually Arise When There is a Need To:

- Pay final expenses (medical and funeral expenses, possible state death taxes, etc.)

- Pay administration expenses including possible tax, legal, appraisal fees, etc.

- Pay off the home, the business or other debts with "discounted dollars."

- Pay at least some estate taxes at the first death in order to:

- Transfer assets valued over the current $650,000 (Unified Transfer Credit) allowance for tax-free transfers to those other than a spouse. **(Remember assets *not passing to the surviving spouse do not qualify for the unlimited marital deduction,* for example, transferring ownership rights in a business to children at the first death.)**

- Minimize the estate tax impact at the second death. Once estate taxes are paid on a portion of an estate, that portion *AND ANY FUTURE APPRECIATION of that portion* of the estate will not be subject to estate taxes at the death of the second spouse.

Finally, both single or joint life policies are valuable for those individuals who want to accumulate large cash values in their policies (which not only grow income-tax deferred at competitive money market rates, but are also free of reinvestment worries and *can even be withdrawn income-tax free by using policy loans offered at favorable interest rates which are much lower than their individual income tax rates).* In these instances, the policy owner has access to these cash values during his/her lifetime for such things as emergencies, opportunities, college funding and to supplement retirement income.[13] (Please read endnote!)

Many individuals, including a great many business owners, have weathered financial storms by borrowing on their insurance when banks wouldn't extend credit. *Policy owners have three choices regarding repayment of policy loans:*

Three choices for repayment are:
• Pay back loan.
• Pay only the interest on the loan.
• Not pay back the loan.

If the third choice is selected, the outstanding loan would be deducted from the death benefit. Another nice benefit is that the policyowner can pay back the loan whenever he or she chooses. However, interest will continue to accrue until the loan is repaid. It is important to point out that, similar to any of your other financial investments, your life insurance coverage—including all your life insurance policies *and any outstanding policy loans*—should be monitored and reviewed with your insurance agent periodically.

The 1% Solution: Perhaps what is most exciting about the use of insurance in estate planning is that *it allows people to save a tremendous amount of money* and for that reason it has frequently been referred to as the 1% Solution.

The way this solution works is that a couple can take approximately 1% of their net worth every year for approximately 10 to 12 years[14] and purchase a second-to-die life insurance policy to fund estate settlement costs and financial needs. The net result is that the couple's total outlay will be only 10% to 12% of the cash required to meet estate expenses!

Imagine, for example, paying only 10 payments of $10,000 each to get a million dollars income-tax-free, precisely when it is needed! By the way, this means, of course, that if the insureds should die at any time during those first 10 to 12 years, their total cash outlay could be substantially less than what was originally projected.

The reason for this is that *life insurance is a unique tool which is able to accomplish what virtually no other product can — in that it is designed to "pay off" whether the policy owner pays only one premium payment or many.*

Therefore, it absolutely eliminates the uncertainty of if there will be *enough time* to accumulate necessary funds! Absolutely no other financial or investment vehicle offers this self-completing feature, and as such, life insurance plays a crucial role in *providing real stability to estate planning.*

In addition, another important self-completing feature available with most policies (for those approximately 55 and younger*) is one which continues to pay the premiums if the insured individual become totally disabled,* thereby offering additional security to the planning process.

Furthermore, there are many separate disability insurance policies all designed to accomplish various objectives — both business and personal — which replace lost income in the event of a disability. This type of insurance protection is extremely important and can play a *CRUCIAL* role in anyone's financial planning!

Life Insurance Outside of the Estate

In order to keep life insurance proceeds out of the estate and thus, avoid federal and state taxation of the death benefit proceeds, it is necessary to make one of the following choices:

Choice #1. Set up an Irrevocable Life Insurance Trust to own the policy or policies. Please note:

- **A REVOCABLE LIVING TRUST,** such as the A-B Trust previously mentioned, *does not* keep your insurance proceeds out of your estate because with a Revocable Living Trust, you *always* have complete control over your assets (to amend, revoke, etc.), and thus, you are considered to have an incidence of ownership in the policy or policies. The *only* type of trust which will prevent your life insurance proceeds from being included in your estate is an Irrevocable Life Insurance Trust.

- **AN IRREVOCABLE LIFE INSURANCE TRUST** can remove the proceeds from the estates of both the insured and the surviving spouse, while making the proceeds fully available to meet the needs of the surviving spouse and the needs of the insured's estate. (The proceeds are available to the surviving spouse ONLY if single life policies are used.)

    PLEASE NOTE, however, that if it is important for the surviving spouse to have access to the insurance proceeds at the death of the first spouse, single life policies or a combination of single life policies and a second-to-die policy should be used.

    If the insureds decide to use a combination of both single and joint life policies in their estate planning, the second-to-die policy should be placed in a separate irrevocable life insurance trust and the surviving spouse must have no incidence of ownership in that policy because he or she is also an insured under a second-to-die policy.

    ALSO, those in community property states may need to do additional planning. In a community property state, ***without an agreement to the contrary***, one half of the proceeds of the insurance policy (even one owned by in irrevocable trust in which the spouse is an income beneficiary) are deemed to be owned by the surviving spouse!

Choice #2. Have an adult child/beneficiary (not the spouse) own the policy. In considering this choice, you should be aware of some possible risks:

- The policies become assets of the children and thus, are subject to the risks of the children's creditors or malpractice claimants.

- Without proper planning, ***if the child predeceases the parents or divorces,*** the policy could become a marital asset and thus, be subject to a divorce settlement or an inheritance by the surviving spouse.

- There is no control over how the children use the money. Therefore, it is important to select this method only when you have a great deal of confidence or trust in the child.

Choice #3. In some instances, Family Split Dollar or Business Split Dollar arrangements can offer dramatic tax leverage and planning opportunities.

Contact your local insurance or legal professional if you would like information about this.

However, it is important to know that if an insured person decides to transfer an *EXISTING* policy or policies to an insurance trust or beneficiary, ***the insured must live for three years for the proceeds to be excluded from the estate.***

New insurance, on the other hand, should be purchased by the trust (with the insured making gifts using the annual exclusion to pay the premiums) or by the beneficiary to avoid an incidence of ownership by the insured.

If you decide to transfer a policy, be sure to obtain advice from a knowledgeable insurance agent or legal adviser. *There can be numerous tax ramifications which need to be addressed!*

What if a Person is Uninsurable?

A big advantage of second-to-die policies is that the underwriting on the policy is considerably more lenient due to the fact that the insurance company will not have to pay out until the death of the second insured.

Therefore, many individuals who would ordinarily have a hard time qualifying for insurance or who would not normally qualify at all, are able to obtain insurance coverage. In addition, there are now also a number of companies which specialize in handling the insurance needs of individuals with health problems that would normally prevent them from obtaining insurance. Thus, many more individuals are able to obtain life insurance than in the past.

However, if an individual still finds that he or she is not insurable, there are still a great many estate planning techniques which can be utilized to help reduce estate settlement costs.

Charitable Giving Techniques

Charitable giving is a very exciting area of estate planning because under the right circumstances it is a **win-win** situation for everyone:

THE DONOR can receive some significant income, gift, and estate tax savings. Gifts made to charity, either during a person's life or at death, reduce the size of the estate and, thus, lower the estate tax liability. In addition, lifetime gifts may also qualify for substantial current income tax deductions.

Charitable gifting techniques are frequently used with gifts of highly appreciated assets to gain tax leverage because these assets, when gifted to a charity, can often qualify for a tax deduction based on the full fair market value of the gifted property. In 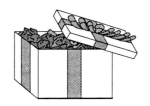 addition, with **deferred gifts** (see below) where a donor retains an interest in the gifted property, donating highly appreciated assets including those that produce little or no income can be very advantageous.

The reason for this is that the charity (which is exempt from paying taxes) can sell the asset, pay no capital gains and reinvest the *entire amount* in investments that may offer a higher yield. AS A RESULT, THE DONOR IS OFTEN ABLE TO

INCREASE HIS OR HER CURRENT CASH FLOW BY USING CHARITABLE GIVING TECHNIQUES!

THE HEIRS, too, benefit in that they may receive an enhanced and/or more *easily distributable inheritance* if the donor decides to use a portion of his/her tax savings to fund a **wealth replacement trust** (see chart below**)** which contains a life insurance policy that will replace (in part, in full or even exceed) with the *cash equivalent value* of what the heirs would have received had no charitable gift been made. This may be particularly valuable if the estate consists primarily of one or more assets that are difficult to divide up equitably among the heirs.

 THE CHARITY, of course, receives the proceeds from your philanthropic gift! In fact, as more advisers and clients become familiar with the many opportunities that exist to solve important income, retirement and estate planning needs through the use of various charitable giving techniques, not only will estate owners benefit a great deal, but also *critical funds* will be made available to schools, churches or synagogues, medical institutions and many other fine and worthy charitable causes!

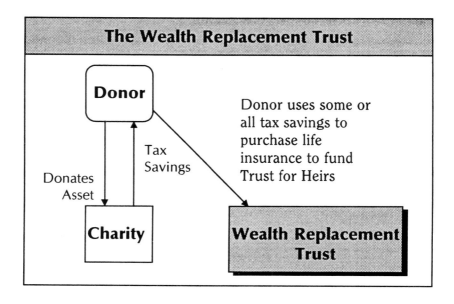

The Wealth Replacement Trust

Donor

Donates Asset

Tax Savings

Charity

Donor uses some or all tax savings to purchase life insurance to fund Trust for Heirs

Wealth Replacement Trust

How Does Charitable Giving Work?

Gifts of cash or other property may be made either during one's lifetime or at death (**testamentary bequests**). They may be either **outright gifts** or **deferred gifts.** Outright gifts give the charity the *immediate* and *full possession* of the gift. Deferred gifts, on the other hand, defer the ultimate gift to charity because the donor retains an interest in the gifted property (and/or gifts that retained interest to another) for a period of time consisting either for the lifetime of one or more beneficiaries or for a term of years not to exceed 20 years.[15]

As mentioned above, charitable giving strategies are used to reduce gift, estate and generation skipping taxes and, in many instances also, to provide generous income-tax savings. Each type of tax and charitable giving technique, however, is governed by its own set of rules. Therefore, it is important to consult with knowledgeable experts in the area of charitable tax planning.

What Charitable Giving Vehicles Can A Donor Choose?

There are *numerous* tools and strategies that can be selected from the "charitable planning tool box." Below is a *very brief* description of various planning vehicles:

CHARITABLE REMAINDER TRUST: A trust established to receive gifts of cash or other property in which the donor reserves the right to receive an income from the trust based on not less than 5% (the donor may choose a higher payout rate) of the fair market value of assets placed in trust for either the life of one or more beneficiaries, or for a term of years not to exceed 20 years. The donor may choose from either a ***CHARITABLE REMAINDER ANNUITY TRUST*** which pays a fixed annuity payout (and allows no additional contributions) or ***CHARITABLE REMAINDER UNITRUST*** which pays an income based on a fixed percentage of the value of the trust assets as revalued annually (and allows subsequent contributions).

CHARITABLE LEAD TRUST: The *opposite* of the charitable remainder trusts. The lead trust provides an income (either an annuity or unitrust interest) **TO THE CHARITY** for either the life of one or more individuals or for a specified term of years (with no 20 year maximum) with the remainder interest either passing back to the donor (a reversionary interest) or to one or more intended beneficiaries.

POOLED INCOME FUNDS: A pooled income fund is a separate trust *maintained by the charitable organization* that is set up to receive contributions from many donors and the property is commingled. The donor transfers cash or other property to the fund and retains a life-income interest (a term of years option is not allowed) in the property for one or more individuals. Payments from the fund to the donor are based on the donor's number of *units of participation* as determined at the time of the gift and the earnings of the entire fund for that year.

CHARITABLE GIFT ANNUITY: A gift annuity does not involve a separate trust. Instead, the donor transfers cash or other property directly to the charity, which, in turn, pays the donor an annuity for life (the annuity is payable over the life of one individual, or the lives of two individuals). The transaction, however, is characterized as both a purchase of an annuity and a charitable contribution in that the value of the property transferred to the charitable organization exceeds the annuity guaranteed by the charity. As a result, the donor receives an income tax deduction based on the *excess of the value of the contribution over the value of the annuity*.

REMAINDER INTERESTS IN A RESIDENCE OR A FARM: The donor transfers title of a personal residence or farm to the charity and retains the right to occupy and otherwise enjoy all beneficial rights in the property for the life of one or more tenants or for a term of years. The gift of the personal residence need not include the *entire* residence *property* nor must a gift of a farm include the *entire* farm acreage.

BARGAIN SALE: A bargain sale is actually a combination of a sale and a gift (and can be made either outright or in trust). This is accomplished by selling an asset to charity *at less than the real fair market value*. Current regulations require the basis in the property to be allocated pro-rata between the sale and the gift. Thus, the donor would realize a gain on the sale portion of the transaction.

FAMILY FOUNDATION: Setting up a family foundation allows the donor and, ultimately, the heirs to *maintain maximum control over the use of the donor's dollars*. There are basically two kinds of family foundations. One is known as a private foundation and since 1969, has been subject to a number of limitations and regulations. The other is known as a **supporting organization** which allows the family foundation to come under the tax and administrative umbrella of a public charity and, thus, qualify as a charity for tax purposes.

Exciting Charitable Giving Solutions

Charitable giving strategies can provide solutions that may not be available through the use of other estate planning techniques. Below are a *few* possible solutions. The donor may:

- Diversify his or her portfolio and avoid capital gains tax on the restructuring of the portfolio.

- Sell a business and avoid capital gains tax on the sale.

- Achieve tax-advantaged solutions for testamentary distributions from pension plans.

- Make a gift to a sibling *and* avoid estate tax in *that sibling's* estate.

- Transform an illiquid asset into an important source of cash for such things as: providing income to dependent parents, paying for a child or grandchild's education, funding long term care needs or purchasing of life insurance, etc.

A Word About Gifts Of Life Insurance To Charitable Organizations

Not only can gifts of life insurance raise *literally millions of dollars* for worthy charities, it is also one of the simplest ways to make a notable contribution. You, as a donor, can derive a great deal of satisfaction knowing that you are making a significant lifetime gift to an important charity you wish to support for a relatively small annual tax-deductible contribution! (You either may donate an existing policy *or* a new policy. Be sure, however, that you comply with your states laws regarding gifts of life insurance to charities.)

In addition to creating a large pool of dollars for a small outlay, life insurance also provides benefits to charities in that:

- There is little administration entailed with a gift of life insurance.

- The charity is spared the delays that wills and trusts may cause.

- There is no shrinkage in the gift due to probate, estate taxes or other fees.

- The charity will not lose the gift if the donor decides to move away.

- During the donor's lifetime, if the need arises, the charity can access the cash values and dividends and, thus, **the policy offers an important source of emergency funds.**

Remember: Life Insurance can turn modest donors into big donors!

Solutions To Federal Gift Taxes

Lifetime gifting is actually a very important tool used in estate planning. For those who can comfortably afford to do so, making gifts during one's lifetime can be one of the best ways to control the onslaught of rapidly increasing estate taxes that result as the estate grows. Also, there are many other reasons why one might want to make gifts to heirs and others during one's life such as:

- To help out loved ones.

- To allow heirs to have the control, use or enjoyment of the asset now.

- To use tax-free or discount transfer opportunities that are available only during life.

- To "give back to society" ***and obtain substantial tax savings*** through the use of charitable gifting techniques.

Therefore, techniques which can help avoid or reduce the transfer costs associated with lifetime gifting are extremely important. Though there are numerous strategies aimed at avoiding or minimizing lifetime gifting transfer taxes, they all boil down to three approaches *that are frequently used in combination with one another to achieve maximum results:*

Lifetime Gifting Which Takes Advantage of Various Gift Tax Credits or Exclusions in Order to <u>Avoid Gift Taxes Entirely</u>.

In addition to the Unified Transfer Tax Credit which allows you to shelter up to $650,000 from either federal gift or estate taxes, there are also four important exceptions to the federal gift tax rules:

1. **Qualified Transfer** — Lifetime payment for either medical expenses or educational tuition *paid directly* to the

educational institution or the medical provider on another's behalf.

2. **Annual Gift Tax Exclusions** — Each year every individual is allowed to give up to $10,000 (married couples can gift $20,000) to as many people as he or she wishes. This amount is now indexed for inflation as a result of the Taxpayer Relief Act of 1997. (State laws vary. Many states either do not have an annual gift tax exclusion or if they do, it excludes less than $10,000.) To qualify for the annual exclusion, gifts must be of "**present interest**" which means the donee must have immediate use and enjoyment of the gift. Gifts made to trusts must meet certain criteria in order to qualify the gift as a gift of "present interest."

3. **The Gift Tax Marital Deduction** — This deduction pertains to gifts of property between spouses. Under current law, AS LONG AS BOTH SPOUSES ARE U.S. CITIZENS, a spouse can give the other spouse any amount of property with no gift tax consequences. Transfers to NON-CITIZEN SPOUSES, however, receive a different tax treatment. (State laws vary and some states have no marital deduction or only a partial marital deduction available for certain gifts.)

4. **The Charitable Deduction** — deduction is allowed for gifts to a qualified charitable organization. Gifts made during the donor's lifetime qualify for a charitable gift tax deduction and, generally, will also qualify for a charitable income tax deduction subject to certain limits (any contributions in excess of allowable limits for the charitable income tax may be carried over and deducted for the next five years). Gifts made at death (testamentary bequests) will qualify for a charitable estate tax deduction.

Gifting Techniques Which Allow the Donor to Transfer Assets at a Discount (Often a Substantial Discount) to Heirs .

Such techniques are often used when transferring a percentage of a piece of real estate (a partial interest) or shares (a minority interest) in a closely held business. These transferred percentages then usually qualify for such discounts as a **partial interest discount, a minority discount** and/or a **lack of marketability discount.**

There are other discounts that have been approved by the IRS, as well, that are not as frequently used or well known as the three above-mentioned discounts. Applying one or more discounts to the property to be gifted can result in some very substantial wealth transfer savings.

In addition, if the donor owns only a minority interest in an asset at death, his or her interest, too, may be eligible for a significant discount!

On the other hand, waiting until death to break up the ownership of an asset into minority interests for heirs *will cause the discounts to be lost.* The reason is that at death, the assets in the decedent's estate are valued as a whole, and not in regard to how they will be separated after death among family members.

FAMILY LIMITED PARTNERSHIPS.

A popular and flexible planning tool that takes discount planning even further is the **family limited partnership.** Utilizing the above-mentioned discounts, **the FLP** enables the senior generation not only to transfer assets at significant discounts, but also to *retain control of those assets even after they have removed them from their taxable estate!*

In addition, **FLP's** may also provide an important layer of asset protection from creditors, lawsuits, and divorce settlements. However, the partnership should be set up before any such problems occur in order to avoid **fraudulent conveyance** rules.

What is a FLP?

It is a limited partnership set up to own various assets (such as shares in a family business, investments, real estate, or other family assets, etc.). Please note that there are certain assets that may not be appropriate for **FLP's**, such as qualified pensions monies, IRAs, annuities and S Corporation stock (an S Corporation may be a partner of an FLP but S stock cannot be contributed as an asset of an FLP — see below.) Therefore, it is important to consult with a competent attorney.

A **family limited partnership** is made up of both **general partners** (usually one or both parents) and **limited partners** (the children and possibly the grandchildren).

In advanced planning situations, the FLP may also have as partners: revocable living trusts, irrevocable life insurance trusts, C or S Corporations, other partnerships, foreign (offshore) trusts, limited liability companies, charitable remainder trusts and private foundations, and/or GRIT's, GRAT's, and GRUT's (GRIT's, GRAT's, and GRUT's are described below).

The **general partners** have complete control and full liability. They also are entitled to a management fee (sometimes calculated as a percentage of the partnership income) and have control over management/investment decisions and income distributions. The **limited partners,** on the other hand, have very restricted control and limited liability.

When the partnership is first drafted, both **general** and **limited partnership interests** are created. For example, 98 LP shares and 2 GP shares. Initially, the parents own all of the partnership interests. Once, however, the assets have been contributed to the partnership, the parents can then begin gifting shares of the limited partnership interests to their children.

The parents may wish to use their annual exclusions to transfer up to $10,000 ($20,000 per couple) of FLP interests per donee per year. They may also decide to use some or all of their $650,000 ($1.25 million per couple) Unified Transfer Tax Credit or even make taxable gifts in order to transfer family wealth, *particularly highly appreciating assets,* more quickly.

These gifted percentages of the limited partnership interests typically will qualify for minority, lack of transferability (limited partners are very restricted in their ability to transfer their shares to anyone else) and lack of marketability discounts. In most instances, qualified appraisals will be required to determine and substantiate the appropriate discounts. Additional costs also may include *annual* limited partnership taxes (in some states) and tax preparation costs. *However, combined discounts may range from approximately 30% to 50%!* What tremendous tax leverage!

GRATs, GRUTs, AND GRITs.

 Another technique to lower gift transfer costs involves the use of certain types of irrevocable trusts where the grantor transfers assets to a trust and retains an interest in the Trust for a period of time (a temporal interest), and at the end of the specified term of years, the trust asset/s pass to the remaindermen (those to whom the remainder interest is being transferred). The reason the asset is ultimately transferred to heirs at a discount is that the remainder interest is a **gift of future interest** and its value is considered less than if the gift had been effective immediately. Thus, the lower valuation results in lower gift taxes. (Since the gift to the remaindermen is a gift of future interest rather than present interest, it does not qualify for the annual gift tax exclusion. Therefore, the grantor either must use some or all of his/her unified transfer credit and/or pay gift taxes.)

These trusts are known as:

- **GRANTOR-RETAINED ANNUITY TRUST (GRAT).** The grantor (transferor) retains an income stream based on a fixed annual payment for a set number of years.

- **GRANTOR-RETAINED UNITRUST (GRUT).** The grantor receives, at least annually, a set percentage of the net fair market value of the trust assets. The value of the trust assets is redetermined every year.

- **GRANTOR-RETAINED INCOME TRUST (GRIT).** This trust may now be used only to transfer a personal residence at a discount and thus, is known as a **personal residence GRIT** or a **personal residence trust (PRIT).** A qualified **personal residence trust (QPRT)** is very similar to the personal residence trust except that its terms are more liberal.

Both the PRIT and the QPRT permit up to two residences (one may be a vacation home). The **PRIT**, however, neither allows any assets other than the residence itself or a fractional interest in the residence to be included in the trust, nor permits the sale of the residence during the term of the trust. A **QPRT**, on the other hand, permits both under certain circumstances.

After the grantor transfers the residence to the trust, he or she retains the right to use (live in) the residence for a term of years, after which the property goes to the persons designated in the trust agreement (the remaindermen).

If, at the end of the term of the trust, the grantor still wishes to live in the home, he or she *must* pay a fair market rental to the remaindermen (*which becomes another way to transfer money to heirs estate tax free!)*. This requirement must be strictly enforced otherwise the entire transaction will be deemed an incomplete gift and *the property will be brought back into the grantor's estate and subject to estate taxes even if gift taxes were paid on the remainder interest gifted to heirs at the origination of the trust!*

The only "catch" to these trusts is that the transferor *must outlive the term of the trust in order for the asset to be excluded from his/her estate. If the transferor dies during the term of the trust, all or a major portion of the trust assets will be included back into his/her estate at the then fair market value.*

However, life insurance on the life of the grantor can be an inexpensive way to guarantee that there will be funds to pay estate taxes if the grantor does not survive the term of the trust. The remainderman (beneficiary) or a separate irrevocable trust should own the policy.

There are huge advantages, however, if the donor does survive the term of the trust. First and foremost, the donor will be able to transfer the asset/s at a greatly reduced gift tax cost (probate is avoided, as well), and as a result, leverage the use of his/her $650,000 Unified Credit. In addition, he/she can effectively "freeze" the value of the transferred asset for estate tax purposes because all future appreciation is passed on to the estate of the donee (remainderman)!

Gifting Which Results in The Payment of Gift Taxes in Order to Transfer Assets Now Rather Than at a Future Date.

Estate owners will frequently opt to transfer assets during their lifetime in order to get highly appreciable assets out of their estate. Also they may wish to allow their heirs to have access to the asset sooner rather than having to wait until the estate owner's death or the death of his or her surviving spouse.

Another very important advantage in choosing to pay gift taxes now rather than estate taxes at death is that, *if the donor lives longer than three years after making the gift,* the **tax** on a lifetime gift actually winds up being much less than a transfer made at death even though gift and estate tax rates are the same. The reason for this is that the gift tax is an exclusive tax and as a result, gifts made during life are only taxed on the amount received by the donee minus the gift tax paid. Estate tax, on the other hand, is an inclusive tax and includes the entire amount transferred as well as the tax paid on that amount.

For example, if the transferor is in a 50% tax bracket and he or she transfers $1,000,000 (over and above the $650,000 protected by the Unified Credit) to an heir at death, the resulting estate tax would be $500,000 and the heirs would receive $500,000. The gift tax on that same asset transferred during life, however, would be $333,333 and the heirs would receive $666,667!

Solutions to Generation Skipping Taxes

Without a doubt, one of the most exciting areas of estate planning centers around the planning opportunities available through generation skipping. No other area offers the potential to transfer literally millions of dollars to successive generations which will be sheltered from BOTH GENERATION SKIPPING TAXES AND ESTATE TAXES in the estates of the succeeding generations! Please note that the transferor will pay either gift or estate taxes. However, *with proper planning*, once gift or estate taxes have been paid, those assets (transferred under the protection of a special generation skipping exemption, see below) *and any future growth* can be sheltered from both estate and generation skipping taxes for *several generations!*

How is This Done?

Though there are a number of sophisticated techniques which can be implemented with regard to generation skipping, there are three basic tools which are used together to protect not only the donor's transfer from generation skipping transfer taxes, but also to accomplish incredible tax savings for future generations and, thus, *minimize the erosion which can occur when each generation must take a big estate tax hit.* The tools are: (1) A $1 million dollar exemption against generation skipping transfer taxes, (2) A Dynasty Trust, and (3) Life insurance and/or other appreciating assets.

The $1 Million Generation Skipping Exemption.

Each person in the United States is entitled to a $1 million exemption **(GSX)** from **Generation Skipping Transfer Taxes** (Married couples can shelter up to $2 million. The $1 million

GSX exemption will be indexed for inflation due to the Taxpayer Relief Act of 1997.)

Please note, however, that there has been some confusion concerning the **GSX** and many people have mistakenly thought that they could transfer $1 million free of any taxes including gift or estate taxes. This is not true.[16] The *GSX is only* an exemption against generation skipping taxes, not gift or estate taxes. Thus, if an individual wanted to transfer $1 million to an heir (either during his/her life or at death), the **Unified Transfer Tax Credit** would shelter the first $650,000 from gift or estate taxes. However, gift or estate taxes would be due on the additional $375,000.

There is a planning technique that allows one to defer estate taxes (but not gift taxes) on the additional $375,000 until the death of the second spouse. For a more detailed discussion of available options, however, it is necessary to seek legal counsel.

The Dynasty Trust and Life Insurance: Maximizing the $1 Million Exemption.

For those wishing to leverage the $1 million generation skipping exemption *into many millions,* the **Dynasty Trust** is the solution!

What is a **Dynasty Trust?** It is an **irrevocable** generation skipping trust (a trust drafted with generation skipping language) which is funded with life insurance and/or other appreciating assets and possibly some discounted assets such as family limited partnership interests..

How Does a Dynasty Trust Work?

Each year the amount necessary to pay the life insurance premium is gifted to the trust and *the GSX is applied to the premium to shelter the premium from generation skipping taxes.* For example, suppose a couple purchased a $5 million policy and paid $50,000 a year for ten years (the approximate time projected for the premiums to "vanish"). *It only "cost" them $500,000 of their GSX ($50,000 X 10 = $500,000) to* *shelter $5 million and all future growth of that $5 million for several generations[17] (which even with conservative growth rates and no extraordinary expenses, could ultimately grow to $40 to $50 million or more!)*

The exemption protects not only the amount of the yearly gift used to pay the insurance premiums, but also the resulting death benefit and all its future growth. Therefore, they could use the rest of their exemption either to purchase additional insurance or to shelter assets in their estate at death.

Actually, at the death of the insured spouse (or the surviving spouse, if a second-to-die policy is used) the trust can use the insurance proceeds to buy back the best assets in the estate for the heirs and future generations.

It is important to realize that, for those who are able and who wish to optimize the use of the generation skipping exemption, TIMELY *lifetime gifting* and the use of life insurance is the key to success! *If one waits till death to apply the GSX to estate assets, the most one can shelter is $1 million ($2 million for couples).* Thus, there will be no opportunity to arrest the inflation of estate assets or leverage the generation skipping exemption.

Other Advantages of a Dynasty Trust

During the children's lifetime, they can have "**sprinkle**" powers. This allows them to have the income from the trust if they need the money and the principal can be invaded for certain major expenses. They can use trust funds for grandchildren's education expenses, medical bills, down payment on a home or a business, etc.

In addition, many estate owners are very much concerned about keeping money and other estate assets *in the family.* This is a legitimate concern considering the high divorce rate and the litigious ("lawsuit crazy") society in which we live. *The advantage of a Dynasty Trust, however, is that in most states, assets owned by a Dynasty Trust are protected from divorce settlements and the children's and grandchildren's, etc., creditors.*

Finally, the trust can employ the services of expert money managers to manage the assets in the trust or name corporate a *co-trustee* (to be a co-trustee with heirs) to help supervise and manage trust assets. This can help prevent financial losses due to immaturity, inexperience, or lack of expertise in financial matters.

Additional Exceptions to the Generation Skipping Transfer Tax Rules.

In addition to the techniques described above, there are also a number of exceptions to the application of the GSTT which allow important planning opportunities:

• Lifetime payment for either medical expenses or educational tuition *paid directly* to the educational institution or the medical provider on another's behalf.

• Gifts within the $10,000 per year annual gift tax exclusion which are given directly to a skip person either outright or in a separate trust for each grandchild or other skip person and which is included in the grandchild's estate (so that the grandchild pays estate taxes at his or her death).

• Transfers made from a trust which are first subject to estate taxes in the children's estate before the grandchildren receive any distributions. Trusts drafted prior to September 25, 1985 that were irrevocable as of that date, are completely exempt from the GSTT. It is important, therefore, not to taint such trusts by adding new property. Irrevocable trusts drafted or added to after September 25, 1985 *should be reviewed to be sure that there is no exposure of trust assets to Generation Skipping Transfer Taxes!!*

• Transfers from a grandparent to a grandchild when *at the time of the gift,* the parent is dead.

Finally, it is important to know that this discussion of Generation Skipping Transfer Taxes is not exhaustive. There is important additional information on this subject which is beyond the scope of this book.

Solutions To Pension Tax Problems

An ENORMOUS AMOUNT OF MONEY which would have been lost to taxes can be saved for your family by TIMELY strategic planning. The best way to do this is to think in terms of "asset relocation and maximization." By wisely repositioning some of your pension assets and taking advantage of the tremendous leveraging capability of life insurance, you can keep a lot more of your money for your family[18].

The way to begin to do this would be to either use funds outside of your pension or IRA accounts or begin taking annual distributions from your retirement plans and[19]:

• Pay the taxes

• Invest the balance, and

• Initiate a lifetime gifting program to get money out of your estate, and thus, lower your estate taxes, and transfer money safely to heirs.

Then, to GREATLY INCREASE the success of your "tax-saving strategy," leverage your dollars and, *SAVE AS MUCH AS 80% to 90% OFF YOUR TAXES*, you can use life insurance to pay your taxes! The way you would do this is:

• Set up an *Irrevocable Life Insurance Trust*

• Gift a portion of the pension proceeds each year to the trust to pay the annual premiums on a life insurance policy for approximately 10 to 12 years (the time estimated for the cash values in the policy to have grown sufficiently to pay the annual premiums). Please see endnote #14.

The result of this strategy is that the insurance benefit, which will be free of income taxes and estate taxes, **can be used to replace the money your family would have lost to taxes!**

Roth IRA Update

The Taxpayer Relief Act of 1997 introduced the new Roth IRA. Beginning in 1998, taxpayers with adjusted gross incomes (AGI) of no more than $95,000 (or no more than $150,000 on a joint return) will be able to contribute up to $2,000 or 100% of compensation annually to a Roth IRA (offset by any contribution made to a regular IRA for that year). The allowable contribution to a Roth IRA is phased out for singles with AGI between $95,000 and $110,000 and for married couples filing jointly, when their AGI is between $150,000 and $160,000. These phase out rules apply whether or not you are an active participant in a qualified retirement plan through work

Unlike regular IRAs, contributions to Roth IRAs are never tax deductible. However, distributions after age 59½ are *completely tax-free* if the Roth has been held over five years. Distributions before age 59½ are also tax-free if the Roth has been held more than five years and the owner dies, becomes disabled, or uses the proceeds (up to a $10,000 lifetime maximum) for a first time home purchase. (*Contributions*, not earnings, can be withdrawn tax-free and penalty-free at any time. Taxpayers are subject to taxes and early-withdrawal penalties *only on distributions in excess* of their original contributions.)

More importantly, the new tax law also allows taxpayers to convert (or roll over) existing regular IRAs into a Roth IRA during any tax year in which their adjusted gross income is *no more* than $100,000. This $100,000 limit applies both to single and married taxpayers filing a joint return. Married individuals filing separate returns are ineligible for the conversion privilege at any income level. Non-deductible contributions from a regular IRA may not be rolled over.

The conversion of a regular IRA into a Roth IRA will cause the amount converted to be included in the taxpayer's gross income for the year of the conversion and, thus, subject to income taxes. (The amount rolled over will not count toward determining the taxpayer's $100,000 AGI limit.) However, converting some or all of a regular IRA to a Roth can have very significant income and estate tax advantages including:

- **Continued income tax deferral after age 70 ½.** Unlike regular IRAs and pension assets which require mandatory distributions at age 70 ½, there are no mandatory distributions requirements associated with Roth IRAs. Also, regular IRAs do not allow any further contributions after age 70 ½, while Roth IRAs do allow further contributions as long as you have earned income. This can allow significant tax-free growth and compounding to occur after the point at which required minimum distributions would have been required under an ordinary IRA. For those who don't need to tap into their IRAs, the additional growth offered by withdrawing little or nothing for as long as possible adds tremendous value.

- **Heirs receive distributions tax free.** If an IRA owner sets it up properly, heirs can take distributions out over a period of years or even over their life expectancy. After the husband and wife die, the beneficiary usually is a child or a grandchild. It's not unusual for such a beneficiary to have a life expectancy of anywhere from 30 to 60 years. The beneficiary can take annual distributions tax-free and leave the balance of the account to grow and compound!

- **FOR 1998 ONLY, the payment of taxes associated with the conversion can be spread out over a 4 year period.** For example, if someone were to rollover a $100,000 regular IRA to a Roth IRA before 1999, though the entire $100,000 is taxable, the taxpayer would be allowed to spread the income over four years (reporting, in this instance, $25,000 of income each year between 1998 and 2001.) In addition, the 10% penalty that normally applies to pre-age 59 ½ distributions does not apply to a rollover to a Roth IRA (made in any year).

To determine if converting to a Roth IRA would be appropriate for you, please consult a qualified financial advisor.

Solutions to Business Continuation Concerns

The solutions to transferring a business successfully and developing a well-coordinated overall estate plan will vary a great deal depending on many factors. Such factors may include: the size of the business, its growth rate, the type of business ownership (sole proprietorship, partnership, C or S corporation, professional corporation or partnership or limited liability company), the percentage of ownership (and cost basis) of each of the businessowners, *the citizenship of each businessowner and that of his or her spouse*, any prior business or estate planning that may have been done, etc. Basically, all the relevant facts and objectives of the business, the businessowners, and their family members need to be taken into consideration in order to draft an effective plan.

Once a well-thought out business succession and estate plan has been designed, it is essential to have it reviewed and updated periodically to make certain that it continues to meet the requirements of any changes in tax laws or in business or personal circumstances.

Below is a brief discussion of some of the various tools and techniques that businessowners have available to them. It should be pointed out, however, that not all tools or techniques are appropriate for any one business or businessowner. Each has its own rules and tax consequences. *Therefore, it is important to consult with advisers who are knowledgeable with regard to business succession planning.*

The Taxpayer Relief Act of 1997

Effective December 31, 1997, *qualifying* owners of family owned businesses will be able to exclude up to $1.3 million (couples can shelter $2.6 million) from estate taxes. The exemption is actually only the difference between $1,300,000 and the applicable exclusion amount. For example, for 1999 it's $1,300,000-$650,000=$650,000; in 2000 and 2001 it's $1,300,000-$675,000= 625,000 and so forth.

To qualify for this exemption:

- The business must comprise 50% of the decedent's adjusted gross estate (including all prior gifts of the business).

- Qualified heirs must inherit the business.

- The family must have owned and material participated in the business for at least 5 of last 8 years.

- 50% of the business must be owned by the decedent and/or family (or 70% owned by two families or 90% owned by three families, but only if decedent and/or family owned at least 30%).

- Businesses with more than 35% of its adjusted gross income as passive income won't qualify (passive income *less than 35%* still must be excluded from value of the business covered by this exemption).

This exemption is not available for lifetime gifts of a business!

Tax Relief Codes

The IRS does offer businessowners some estate tax relief for those businessowners that will face an estate tax liability. While qualifying for these provisions *requires strict adherence* to the rules, they can offer some valuable planning opportunities. Below is a *very brief description*. Please contact your adviser to obtain information on qualification requirements.

- **IRC 6166:** Allows the estate and generation skipping taxes ATTRIBUTABLE to a closely held business to be paid out over a 14 year period (estate taxes attributable to the NON-BUSINESS ASSETS of the estate are not eligible for this deferral.)

- **IRC 303:** Allows a decedent's estate to sell back enough stock to his or her incorporated business to pay estate and generation skipping taxes, funeral costs and allowable administration expenses without having the sale taxed as a dividend for income tax purposes. As a result, in most instances, the sale will not be subject to income taxes!

- **Alternate Valuation Dates:** Allows the decedent's executor to elect irrevocably to have the decedent's estate valued six months after the decedent's date of death (rather than his or her date of death) or the earlier date that the estate property is sold.

- **Section 2032 (a) Special use valuation for Farm and Business Real Estate:** Allows the decedent's estate to value the farm or business real estate on the basis of *current use* rather than its *highest value and best use*. This current use valuation can reduce the estate by up to $750,000 (now to be indexed for inflation due to the Taxpayer Relief Act of 1997).

Buy-Sell Agreements

Most businessowners want and need to control the decision as to who may buy or own stock or partnership interests in their businesses. (This may be particularly important for family-owned busineses and S Corporations who must protect their S Corporation election). Thus, advisers usually recommend that businessowners have a buy-sell agreement drafted for their business.

A buy-sell agreement (also known as a **shareholder's agreement**) is a legally binding contract that spells out the terms and conditions under which a sale of a businessowner's interest will take place.

Buy-sell agreements for businesses with two or more owners usually include restrictions on the sale of stock or partnership interests to outsiders. These agreements typically require that the owners first offer to sell their stock or partnership interests to the company, the other remaining owners, or both upon the occurrence of certain triggering events such as: the businessowner's receipt of an outside offer to buy, retirement, death, disability, divorce, departure, bankruptcy, or loss of a professional license.[20]

Depending upon how the owners want the buy-sell drafted, the agreement either will require the other parties to buy the offered stock or partnership interests or it will merely give them the option to buy. A buy-sell agreement will also state the agreed-upon price for the sale of the shares or partnership interests. The advantage of setting a fair and agreed-upon price for the business interests *while all the owners are alive and well*, is that it protects everyone's interests, including owners with a minority interest in the business. Also, *it prevents or at least minimizes the potential for any later disputes or litigation.*

The agreement should be kept up-to-date and reflect the fair market value of the business. In many instances, a well drafted buy-sell agreement can help peg the value of the business for gift and estate taxes purposes and thereby minimize the

potential for an expensive legal battle with the IRS.

If you own a family business, however, it is important to know that the IRS views transfers of business interests between family members as *naturally suspect*. In fact, tax law changes that went into effect Oct. 8, 1990 made pegging the value of

family businesses for gift and estate tax purposes *much* more difficult. Buy-sell agreements drafted *prior* to Oct. 8, 1990 that have not been "substantially modified" since that time are grandfathered. Therefore, *those having a grandfathered buy-sell agreement should seek expert counsel before they make any changes to their buy-sell agreement.*

There are three types of buy-sell agreements. Each has its own own advantages and disadvantages and tax consequences:

- **Stock Redemption:** (or Entity Agreement): A contractual agreement between each businessowner and the business itself whereby the corporation or partnership agrees to buy back the departing or deceased businessowner's agreed-upon number of shares or partnership interests.

- **Cross-Purchase Agreement:** A contractual agreement between or among the businessowners that upon the occurrence of the specified event, each remaining shareholder will buy back the agreed-upon portion of the stock of the departing or deceased shareholder.

- **Hybrid, A "Wait and See" Buy-Sell Agreement:** A hybrid agreement is usually implemented when the owners desire additional flexibility. This contractual arrangement among the businessowners and the company allows the parties to wait until the triggering event occurs and then decide whether the company, the remaining businessowners or both will buy the departing or deceased businessowner's interest.

As mentioned in the Problems section, *it is essential to seek expert counsel regarding the choice, implementation, or change of any buy-sell agreement.*

Funding Alternatives For Buy-Sell Agreements

Once the buy-sell has been drafted, the owners need to give serious consideration to how they intend to finance or pay for the buy-out of the departing owner's stock. Typically, the alternatives that are available to the remaining owners are to:

- **Pay Cash,**

- **Borrow the Money** (and pay interest *which may or may not be deductible*),

- **Arrange for an Installment Buy-Out** (and pay interest *which may or may not be deductible*), or

- **Purchase Life Insurance and Disability Buy-Out Insurance.**

Paying cash, borrowing the money, or paying off the loan under an installment sale are the most expensive (and often riskiest) methods to pay for the repurchase of a deceased or disabled owner's stock. If, however, life insurance and disability buy-out insurance is selected, the cost of purchasing a disabled or deceased owner's stock will be *discounted significantly* and *all parties will be protected by the assurance that the cash will be there exactly when it is needed!*

As you will see in the chart that follows, the cost of life insurance often will be ***LESS THAN JUST THE INTEREST on the loan!***

For Example: The Cost of Borrowing $100,000 vs Life Insurance

Borrowing $100,000			
Loan Repaid Over	**Interest Rate**	**Annual Payment**	**Total Payments**
10 years	10%	$16,275	$162,750
	12%	$17,699	$176,990
15 years	10%	$13,148	$197,220
	12%	$14,683	$220,254
Life Insurance on $100,000 Policy			
Premiums Paid	**Age**	**Annual Premium**	**Total Premiums**
On $100,000 Policy For (Approximately) 10 Years	35/male	$1,200	$12,000
	45/male	$2,000	$24,000
	55/male	$3,000	$36,000

Life Insurance costs will vary depending upon the amount of insurance purchased, the type of policy selected (single or joint life policies, term, whole life, universal life, variable life, etc.) and the age, sex, health, and lifestyle (smoker/non-smoker, hazardous vocations or hobbies, etc.) of the proposed insured.

If a **lifetime buy-out** occurs, the cash values of the life insurance policy on the departing owner may be used to help fund the lifetime buy-out (if a permanent, cash value policy rather than a term policy is used).

Please note that life insurance used to fund buy-sell agreements has different tax consequences depending upon: (1) the type of buy-sell agreement used (2) the form of business ownership (sole proprietor, partnership, C or S Corp, etc.) and in some instances, (3) whether any of the businessowers own 51% or more of the business. *Thus, the life insurance funding must be carefully coordinated with the buy-sell planning.*

A particularly important benefit of funding a buy-sell agreement with disability insurance (even partially with a small policy) is that the insurance contract will act as an objective third party that defines *when a businessowner is disabled* and helps set the terms of the buy-out. This offers protection to all and minimizes potential disputes and lawsuits.

Please note that disability is not a *remote* risk. In fact, a serious disability, particularly one due to an illness (such as a stroke, cancer, or heart failure, etc.) is much more likely to occur during one's working life than death.

Many businessowners today are taking advantage of two important techniques that enable them to have their companies to pay for a portion or all of the premiums of life and disability insurance. The techniques are called Split dollar and Bonus 162 plans. *Consult with your adviser to see how Your company may be able to pay for the premiums for both your business and personal insurance needs!*

Key Person Life and Disability Insurance and Business Overhead Insurance

Often businesses will purchase either **key person life insurance**, **key person disability insurance** *or both* on the key businessowners or employees in order to indemnify the company against the loss of a key individual to their operation. Such an individual(s) may provide essential product design, sales, managerial, technical or financial expertise to the company. A loss of a key person's valuable expertise can strike a disastrous financial blow to a company.

Key person insurance, on the other hand, safeguards the long-term stability of the company, provides a critical infusion of cash, protects the company's creditline, and *"buys the company time"* to readjust and either adapt to a new successor or find a suitable replacement.

Furthermore, key person life insurance often serves *"double duty"* in that also it is frequently used to fund a **stock redemption (entity)** or **hybrid ("wait and see")** buy-sell agreement.

 **Business Overhead Insurance (BOE)** is another type of insurance that offers important protection. It is available to companies where the *disability of one or more businessowners* would impair the company's ability to pay the fixed expenses of the business or practice. A **BOE policy** will pay the disabled business owner's share (or a sole owner's entire cost) of such ongoing fixed expenses as salaries, regular monthly mortgage or lease payments, business property taxes, utilities, premiums for malpractice insurance, etc.

Not only does a BOE policy protect a disabled owner from having to try to use personal funds to meet business expenses (which may have a devastating effect on *both* personal and business cash flow), *it can literally mean the difference as to whether a disabled businessowner will have a business to return to when he or she recovers!*

Additional Planning Techniques That Are Used To Solve Business Succession Problems:

Businessowners of large, high net worth, or rapidly appreciating businesses (or large estates) will usually discover that they need to implement additional estate planning techniques — *and as quickly as possible* — -if they are to minimize the havoc that estate taxes will wreak upon their estate, their business succession plans and the financial security of their family.

Though these techniques are used frequently in planning for the larger estates, many also may be used in smaller estates. *Please consult with a knowledgeable adviser regarding the advisability and implementation of any of the following:*

- **FAMILY LIMITED PARTNERSHIPS:** Enables the businessowner to transfer assets to heirs at significant discounts and retain control of those assets even after they have removed them from their taxable estate! (See page 82.)

- **RECAPITALIZATION OF CORPORATION (OR PARTNERSHIP):** Enables the businessowner to pass on the future appreciation of the business and still maintain control of the business. For example, in a **recapitalization of *a corporation***, the senior owner's common stock is exchanged for a combination of voting preferred stock (which has a *fixed liquidation value* and pays a *cumulative* **dividend**) and one or more classes of common stock which may be nonvoting or have limited voting rights. The nonvoting stock is subsequently gifted or sold to the children or others.

  In the **recapitalization of a partnership**, the partnership interests are restructured and the senior owners retain partnership interests that control the management of the business, have a *fixed liquidation value* and pays them preferred profit distributions.

- **GRANTOR RETAINED ANNUITY TRUSTS:** Enables the businessowner to transfer assets (or the appreciation of assets) to heirs at significant discounts. (See page 84).

- **CHARITABLE GIVING TECHNIQUES:** Enables the businessowner to sell the business in a tax-advantaged manner and *make a significant contribution to charity*. (See page 74)

- **EMPLOYEE STOCK OWNERSHIP PLANS:** A qualified retirement plan for employees that is invested primarily in the corporation's stock. Stock, rather than cash, may be contributed on a tax- deductible basis — *thus, securing income tax deductions for an employer with little or no cash outlay.* ESOPs often are used to secure funds for corporate growth and expansion with pre-tax dollars, pay for life insurance on key owners and employees with pre-tax dollars, and facilitate the buy-out of owner-stockholders.

- **PRIVATE ANNUITIES:** Enables the businessowner to transfer the business interest (and all future appreciation)

- *out of his or her taxable estate* in exchange for a *lifetime income* paid by the tranferee.

- **INSTALLMENT SALES:** Enables business owner to "freeze" the value of his business interest and transfer the future appreciation to the transferee (usually a family member) through an installment sale. You may also want to ask your adviser about a **Self-Cancelling Installment Note (SCIN)** which is an installment sale that by its terms is extinguished at the death of the seller-creditor.

GLOSSARY

Annual Gift Tax Exclusion:

Each year every person is allowed to give up to $10,000 per person (married couple's can give up to $20,000) to as many individuals as he or she would like. The only stipulation is that the gift must be one of "present interest" — that is, the donee must be given an immediate right to possession or enjoyment of the gift.

Bargain sale:

A bargain sale is a combination of a sale and a gift to a charity. This is accomplished by selling an asset to charity at less than the fair market value.

Beneficiary:

One who inherits a share or part of a decedent's estate or one who takes a beneficial interest under a trust.

Basis:

The original amount paid to acquire an asset. For example, the amount paid to purchase a home, a work of art, share of stocks or to start a business.

Business Overhead Insurance (BOE):

A type of insurance that pays the disabled business owner's share (or the sole owner's entire cost) of the ongoing fixed expenses of the business or practice.

Buy Sell Agreement:

It is a legally binding contract that spells out the terms and conditions under which a sale of a businessowner's interest will take place. Buy-sell agreements for businesses with two or more owners usually include restrictions on the sale of stock or partnership interests to outsiders.

Charitable Deduction:

A tax deduction allowed for a gift to a qualified charitable organization.

Charitable Gift Annuity:

The donor transfers cash or other property directly to the charity which in turns pays the donor an annuity for life. The value of the property transferred **exceeds** the annuity guaranteed by the charity. Thus, the donor receives an income tax deduction based on *the excess value of the contribution* over the value of the annuity.

Charitable Lead Trust:

A trust that provides an income to a charity for a specified period of time with the remainder interest either passing back to the donor or to one or more beneficiaries of the donor.

Charitable Remainder Trust (CRT):

The donation of property or money to a charity, where the donor reserves the right to use the property or to receive income from it for a specified period of time. When the agreed-upon period is over, the property belongs to the charitable organization. The donor in turn receives various tax deductions and tax advantages.

Community property:

Property that is acquired by a husband and wife during their marriage. (In most state gifts and inheritances are excluded.) Spouses have one-half interest in their community property and therefore each may will their half to chosen beneficiaries.

Conservatorship:

A legal process by which the court appoints someone to act as a conservator and be responsible for the assets of an individual who is no longer mentally competent.

Direct Skip:

The transfer of assets or gifts made directly to second-generation beneficiaries, skipping the middle generation. For example, a gift by a grandfather to a grandchild.

Donee:

The recipient of a gift. This may also refer to a recipient of a power of appointment.

Donor:

A person who makes gifts or grants a power of appointment. For example, an individual who donates money or other assets to family members, friends or qualified charities. This also includes an individual who a power of appointment to another individual.

Dynasty Trust:

An irrevocable generation skipping trust (a trust drafted with generation skipping language) which is funded with life insurance and other assets which is designed to create nontaxable generation-skipping transfers to several generations.

Estate Tax:

A tax imposed upon the right of a person to transfer property at death. This type of tax is imposed not only by the federal government but also by a number of states.

Family Foundation:

A foundation set up for charitable purposes which enables a family to maintain maximum control over the use of the donor's dollars. There are basically two types of family foundations. One is known as a private foundation and since 1969 has been subject to a number of limitations and regulations. The other is known as a *supporting organization* which allows the family foundation to come under the tax and administrative umbrella of a public charity and, thus, qualify as a charity for tax purposes.

Family Limited Partnership (FLP):

A legal entity that enables the senior generation to transfer assets at a discount during life to heirs and still retain control of the assets after they have been removed from their taxable estate. The FLP may also provide an important layer of asset protection.

Generation Skipping Transfer Tax (GSTT):

This is a flat 55% tax levied on any transfers (either during one's lifetime or at death) made to heirs or others at least two generations below the transferor (for example, grandchildren, grandnieces/nephews, etc.) The GSTT is assessed in *addition* to any other taxes (such as gift or estate taxes) owing!

Generation Skipping Exemption (GSX):

Each person making a generation skipping transfer is provided under the law with a $1 million exemption from Generation Skipping Transfer Taxes.

Gift Tax:

A tax imposed upon the right of a person to transfer assets during his/her lifetime. Gift taxes can be imposed not only by the federal government but by states, as well.

GRITs, GRATs, and GRUTs:

Grantor retained income trusts, grantor retained annuity trusts, and grantor retained unit trusts are irrevocable trusts where the grantor transfers assets to a trust and retains an interest in the trust for a period of time and at the end of the specified term of years, the remaining trust assets pass to the remaindermen (typically, the grantors heirs). These types of trusts enable the grantor to transfer assets to heirs at a discount. However, the grantor must survive the term of the trust in order for the assets in the trust to be excluded from his or her estate. The transferred assets are considered gifts of future interest and do not qualify for the annual exclusion.

Guardian:

A person named to represent the interests of minor children, whether named in a will or appointed by a court.

Irrevocable Life Insurance Trust:

An irrevocable trust that is established for the purpose of excluding life-insurance proceeds from the estate of the insured for estate tax purposes.

Irrevocable Trust:

A trust created for the permanent transfer of property. Unlike a revocable trust, the irrevocable trust cannot be changed or revoked by the person who created it.

Joint First-to-Die Insurance:

A life insurance policy that covers two or more lives and pays at the first death.

Joint Second-to-Die Insurance:

A life insurance policy that covers two lives and pays at the second death.

Joint Tenancy:

When two or more people own the same property at the same time in equal shares, with the understanding that on the death of any one, the survivor(s) will own the whole.

Living Trust:

A trust created during the lifetime of the grantor. (See also: Revocable Trust.)

Key Person Life and Disability Insurance:

Often businesses will purchase either key person life, key person disability insurance or both on the key businessowners or employees in order to indemnify the company against the loss of a key individual to their operation.

Long Term Care Insurance:

A type of insurance designed to pay the costs associated with long term care.

Marital Deduction:

A deduction for estate or gift tax purposes for the amount of property that passes to a spouse. Under federal law, there is a complete interspousal exemption for qualifying transfers.

Medicaid (known as Medical in California):

It is a form of welfare. In regards to long term care, Medicaid will cover long term care costs only if the ill person's income is insufficient to pay for nursing home costs and he or she has no other means to pay for long term care.

Pour-over will:

A will used in conjunction with a revocable living trust to "pour over" any assets that are not transferred to the trust prior to death. Assets transferred with the pour over will, however, will *not* avoid probate.

Probate:

A legal process by which a person's assets are transferred to beneficiaries according to the provisions of the person's will or as determined by the state (if the person dies without a will.)

QTIP Trust:

(Known as A Qualified Terminable Interest Property Trust.) A trust that enables the donor spouse to qualify assets over the Unified Transfer Tax Credit amount for the unlimited marital deduction (and thus, defer estate taxes until the second spouse dies,) *and still retain the power to designate who will receive the property remaining in the trust at the surviving spouse's death.* To qualify for the unlimited marital deduction, the donee spouse must receive all the *income* from the trust each year for life (and the executor must, at the death of the *donor* spouse, make an irrevocable election to have the property qualify for the marital deduction.)

Remainder Interest in a Residence or a Farm:

The gift of a personal residence or a farm to a charity where the donor retains the right to occupy and otherwise enjoy all beneficial rights in the property for life or a term of years.

Revocable Trust:

A trust that can be changed or terminated during the grantor's lifetime and the property recovered.

Second-to-Die or Survivorship Life Insurance:

See joint second-to-die insurance.

Trust:

A legal arrangement under which one person (the trustee) controls property or assets put into the trust by another (the trustor) for the benefit of a third person (the beneficiary). The same person can be all three.

Unified Transfer Tax Credit:

A credit that is available to every individual and which is applied against both the gift and estate tax. The amount of the credit is $202,050 and will offset the transfer tax on total taxable transfers of $625,000.

Uniform Probate Code:

A provision which allows owners of certificates of deposit, savings accounts and checking accounts to set up their accounts in a manner which will allow the assets to avoid probate when the assets are transferred to heirs at the owners' death. A number of states have adopted the uniform probate code and additional states are considering the adoption of this code.

Unlimited Marital Deduction:

See Marital Deduction.

Wealth Replacement Trust:

An irrevocable life insurance trust that owns a life insurance policy on the life of a charitable donor. The proceeds of the life insurance policy will be used to replace the value of assets gifted to charities for the heirs of the donor.

Will:

A legally binding document with instructions for the disposition of one's property at death. A will can be amended or revoked up to the time of death or until there is a loss of mental capacity to make a valid will. A will must be enforced through the probate court and, thus, does not avoid probate.

Endnotes

---

[1] Currently, the Federal Estate Tax Exemption excludes estates under $650,000 from federal estate taxes.

[2] (This point applies only to married couples living in a community property state. Laws concerning a step-up in basis vary in separate property states. Therefore, it is important to consult with local legal counsel.)

[3] The Taxpayer Relief Act of 1997 introduced the new capital gains provision which allows a $250,000 ($500,000 if married and filing jointly) capital gains exclusion from for the sale of a principal residence (that has been owner occupied for at least two of the last five years).

[3] Custodial care helps a person perform activities of daily living (ADLs) which include assistance with eating, bathing, dressing, toileting and other routine activities.

[5] (a) Unless a six-month extension is granted (or a longer extension is allowed due to some limited hardship exceptions). (b) The only other exception available is one that allows only the portion of taxes attributable to a closely held business to be extended over 14 years (however, interest is then tacked on to the estate tax bill.) [IRC Section 6166] To qualify, the business must comprise more than 35% of the decedent's adjusted gross estate and the business (or farm) must continue to be operated by "qualified persons" (members of the decedent's family.) A sale to someone other than a "qualified person" will cause the deferral to terminate.

[6] Pension monies may also be subjected to generation skipping taxes on any portion of those monies gifted or bequeathed to those at least two generations below the donor! This tax is a flat 55% and is assessed in addition to any other taxes owing!

[7] The Tax Reform Act of 1984 eliminated the estate tax exclusions for benefits payable under a qualified plan. Retirees who had begun receiving their benefits prior to 1983 and who had irrevocably elected the form of benefit the beneficiary were eligible to have their plans exempted from estate taxes. Those who met the above qualifications prior to January 1, 1985 were able to exclude $100,000 of their plan assets.

[8] In an effort to keep this manual brief, I have not included detailed discussion of living trusts. However, there are a number of outstanding texts on the living trust in local bookstores.

[9] Please note that there are some instances in which a living trust does not avoid probate, such as when there is any litigation involving the estate, either in process at the time of death or as a result of death (wrongful death suit), or if there is a tax audit being conducted.

[10] While a living trust can be used to oversee property for a minor, *the court must still appoint a guardian for any minor.* However, when one has a will and a living trust, the whole process is speeded up and simplified.

[11] Please note that under the new laws, with limited exceptions, every state has the power to go after the estate of Medicaid recipients. This includes the ability place a lien on the ill person's home after his or her death (or that of his or her spouse) in order to recover nursing home costs!

[12] Many states either do not have an annual gift tax exclusion or if they do, it excludes less than $10,000. Thus, state gift taxes may be assessed.

[13] However, if a policyowner wants to retain control over the cash values or beneficiary designations, he is said to have retained an incidence of ownership in the policy, and thus, the proceeds will be included in his estate for estate tax purposes. There are some limited ways to get around this.

[14] Many policies may be structured so that the policy owner may either pay somewhat lower premiums over his or her lifetime or larger premiums over a period of several years. The later option is available due to the fact that after a period of time, the cash values in the policy, including dividends and/or interest may grow sufficiently to pay the annual premiums.

[15] Recent 1997 tax law changes will prevent charitable remainder trusts **(CRTs)** that are set up for the benefit of younger beneficiaries—such as, those in their early thirties or CRTs that are set up with younger children or grandchildren as beneficiaries or successive beneficiaries—*from qualifying for a charitable deduction. Testamentary* CRTs and *additions* to existing CRTs should be reviewed and amended, if necessary.)

[16] There are some planning situations (but not all) in which the annual gift tax exclusion may be used to avoid gift taxes.

[17] In most states, such a trust is allowed to remain in existence for up to 21 years after the last person to die who was *living at the time* the trust was created. This limitation on trusts is known as the **rule against perpetuities**, which prohibits the establishment of trusts which last indefinitely.

[18] The extent of any gifting program should always be considered in light of the impact that such lifetime gifting will have on the long-term financial security of you and your spouse.

[19] There is a 10 percent penalty on **premature distributions** — distributions made before age 59½ — unless one becomes disabled, dies, or annuitizes the entire contract after separating from employment.

[20] Also, a sole proprietor (or sole owner of an incorporated business) may decide to enter into a **one-way buy-sell agreement** with a key employee, relative or outside third party.